Getting the Message Across

GETTING the MESSAGE ACROSS
Public Relations, Publicity and Working with the Media

SUE WARD

journeyman

LONDON • BOULDER, COLORADO

First published 1992 by Journeyman Press
345 Archway Road, London N6 5AA
and 5500 Central Avenue,
Boulder, Colorado 80301, USA

British Library Cataloguing in Publication Data
A catalogue record for this book is available from the British Library

ISBN 1 85172 042 1 hb
ISBN 1 85172 043 X pb

Produced for Journeyman Press by
Chase Production Services, Chipping Norton
Typeset from the author's disks by
Stanford Desktop Publishing Services, Milton Keynes
Printed in Finland by WSOY

Contents

Part II: Methods of communication

Part IV: The media

Abbreviations

DSS   Department of Social Security
DTI   Department of Trade and Industry
DTP   Desktop Publishing
NAPF National Association of Pension Funds

PART I
Your aims, objectives and strategy

1

Introduction

This book is written for community and campaigning groups, trade unions, and political groups.

It is a practical guide to publicity work, both directly through leaflets, posters and similar material, and indirectly through the press, television and radio. It covers skills such as putting together a leaflet, writing a news release, and giving a radio interview. Most people in campaigning groups will agree that we need to understand these and to improve our techniques here.

It also covers 'public relations' – in particular, how your group's 'image' is created and can be changed, and the way you look to the public in your day to day work.

Public relations is seen by many people as meaning slick commercial techniques, used by people who do not care about the subject but only about getting publicity for whatever they are being paid to publicise, and who are willing to be unscrupulous in the way they do it. Selling a cause 'like a packet of cornflakes' is regarded with great distaste by campaigners.

This is understandable, but it is a mistake to throw away good ideas just because other people misuse them. One particular point made by commercial 'image consultants' is the subject of Chapter 2 of this book. This is that *everything* you do affects the way you are seen by the public and therefore influences whether you are able to get your message across. If, for example, you claim to be an efficient and caring organisation but there is never anyone answering your phone, or it is answered in a curt way that suggests the public are a nuisance, you simply will not be believed. Campaigning groups are often too busy or stressed to think about this, or do not regard it as important enough.

This book, then, is about how to get over to people what your policies and ideas are and convince them that they are right.

There are three main reasons for reading it. You could be:

* A group providing a service or giving information about problems that won't go away, for instance about homelessness or a particular illness. You may receive a continuing flow of media interest, or

you could have decided that you want to increase the number of people who hear about you, and get them to think about you.

- A group running what you hope will be a short campaign, perhaps to defend a hospital or a school, or persuade the authorities of the need for something new. You will be working intensively over a few months or so, perhaps with a definite 'make or break' date in front of you.

- A group that has suddenly been plunged into dealing with the media, because a crisis has blown up – perhaps a strike, a scandal in your organisation, or a celebrity or major politician who is about to descend on you. You could even have reporters and photographers on your doorstep for as long as the crisis lasts.

This book is intended to give help in all these, and any other situations in which you have to deal with the media, and also to help any group that wants to produce a leaflet or newsletter, or any other piece of publicity. The overall message is that you will do better if you work out what you are doing and why. Even in a crisis, it's worth taking the time to think about your basic message and to plan a framework and timetable for dealing with the media. Chapters 2–6 are intended to help you do this and to find the skills and resources you need.

In Chapter 4 there is an outline of the different methods of publicity, their advantages and disadvantages, and the ways you can use them. Each of the following individual chapters looks at the practical issues surrounding the various methods, and how to use them effectively. There are a number of checklists and worksheets to help plan your work.

Publicity work, of course, does not stand on its own. The idea for this book came while I was writing another one, also published by Pluto Press, called *Organising Things*. This is about setting up and running all sorts of events, from the national demonstration to the small public meeting. The two books fit together in many ways. One is about running the events, the other is about publicising them. So it is hoped that people will look at both. There are other books covering some of the subjects in this book, and they are listed in Appendix 1: Booklist.

A warning

This book is being written at the beginning of the 1990s. The equivalent book published at the beginning of the 1980s, Denis MacShane's *Using the Media* is well worth reading, but looks distinctly dated now. There has been more than a decade of Tory government, and many changed attitudes. There have been major changes in technology, with electronic news gathering, the spread of videos and computers, and the introduction of desktop publishing. The press, too, has changed character, with the arrival on the scene of barons such as Rupert Murdoch, the appearance of weekly and daily 'free' newspapers and the decline of investigative journalism.

The public has also become used to much better quality, slicker advertising and publicity material from all sorts of sources. The tatty duplicated leaflet that would just about do ten years ago will be thrown away unread today.

There will be other changes in the next decade. In ten years' time we may be thinking quite differently about every subject covered in this book. The advice included here should not be followed slavishly. In any event, what works well in Surrey today may not be right for the Shetlands.

So use it as a guide and a starting point. But in this, as in much else that concerns relations with the public, the key point is to *think things out*.

2

Who are you and what are you doing?

There is a well known sentence about 'no publicity is bad publicity.' Like a lot of such sayings, this is not true. You can find that you are getting a lot of publicity, but that it is all bad for your organisation – because it shows it in a bad light, or because it is not helping you to achieve your aims, or because it is working in the opposite direction to those aims.

For example, organisations that work with people with disabilities are today generally committed to the idea that they should help their clients to be as independent as possible, rather than treating them as objects of pity. So every time an advertisement or story appears in the papers showing a person with a disability as helpless or pitiable, it's a setback for these organisations. The publicity may be 'good' in the sense that it raises money – but it does so by contradicting what the organisation stands for.

It is easy to be trapped in this way, especially since journalists tend to be on the look-out for 'easy' stories that fit in with standard ideas. If you want to create a new or different picture of the group or the cause you represent, you have to work to ensure that the publicity you get fits in with your aims.

It's often also easy to obtain publicity that is not actually bad, but is limited in its usefulness because it only reaches those who already know about the issue and are converted, without touching the people you have to influence. A good publicity campaign will do *both*. Telling your supporters what is going on and where you have succeeded, will keep them feeling happy and committed, but the material you are using for this sort of story should come from the publicity you are doing elsewhere.

To avoid falling into these publicity traps, you need to know what your aims are and what the aims of your publicity work are.

A statement of aims

The first step is to work out a 'statement of aims' (sometimes also called a 'mission statement'). This is an explanation of what your organisation exists *for*. Only when you know this can you know what is good and what is bad for you.

Many groups find it difficult to put together such a statement. The members will be heavily concerned with what the group *does*. The statement of aims, though, is trying to get beyond that, and explain *why* it does so. Groups do not campaign or provide a service just for the sake of doing so: they do it for a reason. Shelter, for instance, campaigns for homeless people because it wants them to be able to live in decent accommodation. That means it must think critically about how 'housing' comes into being and is used.

Most of the larger national organisations have worked out a statement of this sort already. If there's not one available, ask why. You could perhaps send your statement, when you have worked it out, to your parent body and suggest they adopt it too, or tell you what is wrong with it.

An example

Here is an example of the kind of statement you are looking for. It's the one worked out by the Elmbank Action Group, an imaginary group who are going to be used for case studies in a number of places in this book. They are a parents' group, formed after a child at one of the local schools was knocked down by a car at a dangerous road junction. They decide that their purpose is:

To ensure that our children can get to and from Elmbank School safely, without being in danger from speeding traffic.

As you'll see, this sentence is not specific; it does not say what measures they want taken to make the roads safer. The group know what they want; a traffic island in the middle of the road and a 'School' sign before the junction. But they are trying to keep firmly in their minds the idea that these are means to an end, ways of fulfilling their aim rather than the aim itself. Someone might come up with better ideas about how to deal with the speeding traffic and the group could adopt them without harming their purpose.

Do you need publicity at all?

Having worked out what your *group* is for, you next need to work out whether you need publicity at all. Will it help you to achieve your aims, or will it create more difficulties?

Reasons for rejecting publicity might be:

– because you are in the middle of negotiations, for instance on a new pay deal or procedure agreement in your workplace, and the situation is changing every day;

- because you think publicity might harden the attitudes of a certain group that you are trying to win over, such as management in a workplace dispute, or local residents hostile to a new project;
- because you are afraid you'll be swamped by demand for your work – for instance, if you are an underfunded Rape Crisis Centre; or
- because you are dealing with the personal problems of a small group of people and publicity could identify and, therefore, embarrass or distress them.

If you are in this position, you may still need to think about your strategy for *not* publicising yourselves and how you will react if someone wants to write a story about you. You might, for instance, need to build up good relations with one or two newspaper editors so that they understand your problems and know you will offer them stories when it *is* appropriate.

If you do want publicity

If you decide you do want publicity, think next about what it is for.

Use the same method, of finding a single sentence, or perhaps a couple of sentences, which spell out exactly what you are after. Your 'publicity statement' should tell you:

- what you are trying to say;
- who you are trying to reach;
- what you want them to do; and
- on what timescale.

So the Elmbank Action Group's sentence would read:

To make people in the area aware of the dangers of the road junction near Elmbank School, so that they will pressurise the councillors to bring in safety measures this year.

If you break this down, it covers all the necessary points:

what you are trying to say	that the road is dangerous
who you are trying to reach	people in the area
what you want them to do	so that they will put pressure on councillors
and on what timescale	this year

If you are part of a national group there may already be a statement like this worked out. So think about how to adapt it for your level. You won't have the need or resources to deal with every MP in the country, for instance. You might want to put pressure on just one MP instead, or a particular council.

Your audience

The next step is to look at your 'audience' more closely, to decide who they are, and what smaller groups they comprise. This is important, because – as the next chapter shows – the most *efficient* and *effective* methods of communication will be different for different groups.

The audience could be a very large group, or quite a small one. Political parties, for instance, are trying to reach and persuade everyone who has a vote to be used in a general election, but shop stewards trying to achieve a 'yes' vote in a ballot on industrial action need only reach the few hundred people who are involved in that bargaining group.

For many organisations there is a very small group, even just one person, who will make the final decision on the issue that you are interested in. But order to reach that person, you may need to go through other people and to get them to exert pressure on that ultimate target.

So a group campaigning against a school closure, for instance, needs to influence the Secretary of State for Education so that he or she will not agree to the proposal. But they can't do this directly, as it's very unlikely that they will actually get to see him or her. If they did, their voices alone would not carry enough weight. So they need to influence several other groups to bring pressure to bear. These would include:

- the local councillors;
- the local MP;
- the teachers and their staff at the school;
- the rest of the parents at the school;
- parents in other schools which might be under threat;
- anyone else in the area who might be willing to write to the MP about the issue and/or change their votes as a result.

Some of these groups are themselves decision makers, like the local councillors; others are those who can influence the decision-makers, like the school parents, the other parents, the rest of the general public, the council officers and the backbench MPs.

Sub groups
Often your audience will have one thing in common – their voting power or their membership of a trade union – but a lot of things that

are different. Some will vote Tory, some Labour; some will be men, some women; some will be black, some white, and so on. There will also be differences in people's attitudes. A trade union balloting on industrial action, for instance will have among the audience:

–   people who are strongly in favour, who could help or hinder the cause by the way they pass on the message;
–   people who are strongly opposed, who could damage (by their mistakes) or help your cause by what they say; and
–   people who are uncommitted.

Within each of these groups there will also be certain key people whose opinions are respected by others.

People are going to fall into more than one category. Think what the most important differences between them are, for your purpose.

Groups outside your 'target audience'

No message will ever get over *only* to the people who you want to hear it, and you will never be the only group communicating with them. For instance, the union running a ballot needs to be aware of:

–   husbands, wives, and partners of the members;
–   people they meet socially, in the club or in the pub;
–   other people in the workplace, such as management or those in other unions.

Some of these people will be more important than others: in this example, management would probably be quite influential, the friends in the pub much less so. At the very least, you need to be sure that when you are talking to your specific audience, you don't give 'hostages to fortune', by saying things that other people can use against you later.

The other side

Many people will have someone whom they don't mind offending – the enemy, so to speak. For a political group, for instance, it would be the members of the other parties.

In most campaigns, though, you are going to have to convince some of the other side at least before you can win your cause. In addition, what you say to them is always going to be picked up by other people as well, the ones you *do* want to convince. Being rude to a heckler from an opposition group at a public meeting, or jeering at the councillors on the opposition bench during a heated debate, may make you feel better, but it will be noticed by the rest of the audience, or the people in the public gallery, or even the people running the television cameras. You could find you have made people think, 'Well, if they behave like that I want nothing to do with them,' and so you will have lost support you could have gained.

There is, of course, a place for well-directed anger. The key point is never to lose control of yourself, and to remain strong without being rude. In events like meetings with your local MP, using techniques like having an 'hard' and a 'soft' person in the discussions are likely to be more effective than simply showing your annoyance.

Draw a diagram
One of the best ways to work out who your audiences are is to draw a diagram, or more than one.

Taking the example of the school closure campaign, the decision-makers would be in a circle in the middle, subdivided into those at local level and those at national level. Some of the other audiences would be in a larger circle round it, subdivided into smaller segments, while others would be in a series of smaller ones touching the central one.

The 'outer circle' includes those who are in the same broad category as those in the inner one, but without the same power. Examples are councillors who are not on the Education Committee, or backbench MPs. The separate circles are people that you think will have some influence on the decision makers, like parents at your school and others. Groups who are the 'opposition' could be in the inner or the outer circle, or a separate outside group, depending on what their influence is.

Where are you now?

Think about where you are starting from. What publicity work have you done so far, and how do you look to your target audience? Do you have the image you want to have, and does it reinforce rather than contradict your message?

'Image' may sound like an advertiser's word, but it applies far more widely. Every individual, and every group, creates an image among the people they are in contact with, and this can work for or against the message they are trying to convey.

If people feel that the group is friendly and knows what it is talking about, they are far more likely to listen to your message and be responsive to it than if they feel that it is hostile or that its facts are not to be trusted. The more contact you are asking them to have with you, the more they will want to test you out and establish what you are really like before agreeing.

The image of an organisation
For an organisation, the sort of things that give an impression of its personality to the general public will include:

- The appearance of the office, or the place where you hold meetings.
- The reaction outsiders get when they enquire about you – for example, whether they can find a phone number easily, whether it is answered, and what information they are given.
- The way enquiries are followed up.
- The way group members approach others in the street, on the doorstep or at the workplace.
- The sort of letters sent out by the group.
- The information the group puts out that it controls, like posters, leaflets and newsletters.
- The sort of events at which the public sees the group – public meetings, demonstrations, social occasions.
- Whether these events seem to go smoothly or be chaotic.
- How the group conducts its disagreements – especially if they are in public.
- What the press, television and radio say about the group's personality.

So you need to analyse, and to ask other people, what your group looks like to those outside it. Imagine you are a newcomer to the area, or someone who has just started a job at your workplace. Start from the beginning, when he or she first becomes aware of you, and work through to the point when he or she becomes an activist, as knowledgeable about the organisation as you are. Be self-critical, but constructively so.

Think next about how you would *like* to appear. Most groups would like to be seen as efficient and caring. If you're providing a service – especially to children or elderly people – it will usually be important to be professional also. On the other hand, if you're a protest group or pressure group, being amateur or 'David taking on Goliath' may be part of what you need to get across. Similarly, if you are appealing for money, you will not want to appear too affluent.

It may help to put together a 'snapshot' of yourselves in half a dozen adjectives that you would like people to use to describe you.

Taking the necessary action
You should now be able to draw up a list of points where you need to change. These might range from the design of your leaflets to the way you answer the phone. Link these in with your publicity plan, covered in Chapters 5 and 6.

However, if you find that there is serious disagreement between you, it may be best not to try drawing up a strategy immediately; there could be other problems with your organisation, which need solving first. For instance, people may have very different expectations of what you are going to provide, and this could show through when you start appearing more in public.

You may need to find an outside person – often called a 'consultant' – to come in and work through the problems with you. This should help to ensure that your arguments do not tear the group apart. Alternatively, you could use some of the exercises in the various books available.

Keep things under review

Many groups' campaigns go through a number of stages before finally reaching their goal. The image of the group and the main 'target' audience may also change as time goes on. When a school or hospital is threatened with closure, for instance, the first decision will be taken at local level, by the councillors or the District Health Authority members, but the final decision is taken at the centre, in Whitehall. So the important groups are then the Secretary of State and the MPs who can influence him or her. Think about this at the beginning, when you are planning your strategy, and consider it again later as the campaign develops.

Worksheets

Worksheet 1: What are you trying to do?

---

1. Your 'statement of aims'
Write down in this box (or on a separate sheet of paper) a single sentence which identifies what your group's aims are.

```



```

2. Your 'publicity statement'
Now put down a single sentence – or two at most – which says what the purpose of your publicity is.

```




```

3. To check that you have it right, put down in the boxes beside each question below, the part of your sentence that covers it.

what you're trying to say	
who you're trying to reach	
what you want them to do	
on what timescale	

4. Divide up your audience
Now draw a diagram – or more than one – showing the different groups whom you are trying to reach, and those who will hear the message anyway.

Worksheet 2: Your Image

A. Put yourselves in the shoes of someone coming new to the group. Using the points listed on pages 11–12 as a checklist, summarise in a few sentences what impression you think your organisation would give to them.

```
┌─────────────────────────────────────────────────┐
│                                                 │
│                                                 │
│                                                 │
│                                                 │
│                                                 │
└─────────────────────────────────────────────────┘
```

B. Put down a list of up to six adjectives that you would like to have used to describe your group:

1.
2.
3.
4.
5.
6.

C. Using again the points on pages 11–12 as a checklist, list below any of these aspects that you need to change.

```
┌─────────────────────────────────────────────────┐
│                                                 │
│                                                 │
│                                                 │
│                                                 │
│                                                 │
└─────────────────────────────────────────────────┘
```

Look back at these when you come to draft your 'action plan', as set out on pages 51–7. Make sure that you have included them among the things you are going to do over the period of the plan – preferably, early on.

3

The basic rules of thumb

The key rule

There is one key rule, in any sort of communication. Everything else flows from it.

This rule is *start from where your audience is, not from where you are.* That is, before you ever open your mouth, or put pen to paper, think about:

-   what the people you are trying to reach will be interested in finding out; and
-   what they will already know, and think, about the subject.

It's all too easy, if you are deeply involved in something, to forget that most of the world is not. But you need always to put yourself in the shoes of someone who has only just come on the scene, or who has heard of you but has forgotten everything they knew about the issue since they last read your newsletter.

To succeed in your campaign, you have to convince people that they should take an interest in the matter at all. This means stressing what it will mean for *them*, not what it will mean for you. For instance, a union wanting to protect the street-sweeping services against privatisation might be most interested in saving jobs. But most of the public could not care less whether there were 50 street-sweepers in the town, or only 40. What they do mind about is whether the streets are clean or not, so a campaign addressing the general public needs to talk about the effects on the *service*, not the effects on the *jobs*.

Following on from this principle, there is a series of rules of thumb. To summarise them briefly:

-   Concentrate on one main point at a time.
-   Reinforce this main point in several different ways, and through different types of publicity.
-   Find an 'angle' – something that your audience will see as the problem or the opportunity – and offer them a solution or a way of moving forward.

16

- Link what you are saying with people's lives and things they will know about, or want to know.
- Be positive.
- Keep whatever you say brief, simple and straightforward, in ordinary language that's as close as possible to the way people speak.
- Make each item self-contained, so that someone new to the area can understand it.
- If you want people to do something, make it easy for them.
- Tell people who you are.
- Make the most of your opportunities.

One point at a time

Your audience are busy people, and are only going to be willing to take in a certain amount at a time. If you offer them too long or too complicated a message, you'll annoy or confuse them. So keep the message down to the bare essentials. Make one main point each time, and back it up with arguments and reasons. If you have more than one point to make, then use separate pieces of publicity, or clearly separated sections in a newsletter or a magazine.

When you are planning a piece of publicity work, first of all write down this main point in a single sentence. You can eventually turn it into the sentence you will put at the top of your leaflet, the beginning of your newsletter article, or at the start of a speech. If you cannot create a sentence, or can only do so by cheating, using 'and' to join two separate points together, think again. Either there isn't a point that can be got across, or you have got more than one.

If it is the first, you need to rethink completely. If it is the second, then split the material up. This might mean writing two separate stories in a newsletter, or producing two press releases or two leaflets. If this is not possible, decide which is the more important or the more topical story. Can the other wait until the next edition of the newsletter, or go into a press release rather than the leaflet? If not, then throw it away – it is less wasteful than having other people do so, after you have sweated over the contents of a leaflet or an article.

Reinforce what you are saying

You have a single main point; but make this in as many different ways as you can. You could use a cartoon that makes the same point as the words in a leaflet, but in a humorous way. Or you could have a picture that shows people what you mean when when you describe someone as 'sleeping on the streets' in a newspaper article.

Try to use several different forms of publicity at once, with the same main point, so that the message hits people in several ways. For instance, if you are holding a public meeting or knocking on people's doors, give them a leaflet to study later and try and put up posters that get the same point across.

Find an angle

The sentence you put together should answer two questions, of the sort an uninterested member of the public might ask. These are: 'so what?' and 'why now?'.

You have to catch the attention of your audience, and persuade them to stay with you. To do this you need to find what newspaper editors call an 'angle'. The point you are making has to be *relevant* to your audience, and it has to be *topical*. Most people are too busy keeping life going from day to day to have much time for abstract ideas or suggestions about what might have been, or for facts that don't seem to have any bearing on their lives.

For example, when the Campaign for Lead Free Air started, it could be reasonably sure that very few people even knew that there was lead in petrol, let alone what harm it did to children's health. So their first step had to be catching their attention. If they had done so by saying, 'Did you know that there was lead in petrol?' most people's reaction would have been 'so what?' Instead, its first message was, 'Did you know that petrol fumes are harming your children's health?' which made people listen because they cared about their children's health.

Relate it to people's lives

The things that matter to most people are very close to them – their family, their friends, their home, their colleagues at work and their workplace, having enough to live on and enjoying themselves at least part of the time.

If a leaflet comes through the door that seems to be about 'education', most people will throw it away. If it's about local schools, they'll look twice at it. If the headline is about local school*children*, and they have a child at school, they may well read on in case it turns out to be important. If it then appears that it's nothing to do with them, they'll probably stop reading it, but if it seems that even though the children concerned are on the other side of town, it could affect theirs as well, they may well carry on.

Look at the stories in today's newspaper. In each one, the reporter has turned the issues and arguments into individual cases, or people who speak from their own experience. A news story will almost always have a quotation from someone – a victim, a professional or expert, or a politician.

Most people like to be able to see what they are talking about in their 'mind's eye'. Abstract ideas and concepts, on the other hand, take effort to work out what they mean.

Use examples

Bring your abstract ideas to life and explain yourself, by using real and imaginary examples. For example, you could explain 'homelessness' by saying that it means:

- living in bed and breakfast accommodation, like Mary who has two small children and must share cooker and lavatory with twenty others; or
- sleeping on a friend's floor, like 16 year old Derek who has been thrown out by his parents and cannot claim Social Security; or
- sleeping rough in a doorway, like Dick who has been without a fixed address since his wife died five years ago ... and so on.

Seeing what could happen to themselves, or someone like them, in the circumstances you're putting over, brings the point home to people.

If you haven't got a real example, invent one – but make clear that that is what you are doing. Make your examples plausible, and make them about people or things that your intended audience might know. For instance, talk about people earning round about the average wage for the area rather than a very low or a very high one, and with two or three children rather than six or seven.

But if the point of your argument is that people in *untypical* circumstances are going to be specially affected, then you must use them as examples to get the point across.

What is 'typical'?

What people think of as 'typical' – for instance, the married man with full time job, living with his wife and two small children in a nice modern house – is not so in fact. Only about 5 per cent of the workforce are men in this category, so the majority of the people you are addressing won't be 'typical'. Pick out your examples and phrase your arguments with this in mind.

Make sure that what you are saying is relevant to women as well as men, older as well as younger people, and also to groups such as single parents and people from ethnic minorities. It's insulting to write or speak for only one of these groups, as if the others did not exist or could not read.

Be positive
Try to get over the message that you are campaigning *for* something good, rather than *against* something bad. Almost all of us feel, at some time or other, that life is miserable enough as it is, without other people coming in from outside to moan. Tell people what can be done to make things better, rather than about what has happened or might be going to happen, to make things worse.

For example, the Labour Party has got the reputation of having no policies, when in fact it has plenty. But what people *hear* is that they go on about how awful life is under the Tories. By the time they get to their own policies, people have switched off.

You can be positive even about a campaign which appears to be about a negative, such as a cut or a closure, if you use the *reasons* as the basis for your campaign. For instance, if you are campaigning to save a school, it will be because you want good local education for your children.

Being positive may only need a conscious change in the words you use – like saying that you are campaigning *for* the school to stay open, rather than *against* its closure. The first message is the more attractive to ordinary people, and it leads naturally to your arguments in defence of the school – that it's providing a good education, that it's local, that the children are happy there.

Being positive also helps when the activity you are trying to defend is not very good, or is unpopular with the public. If, for instance, the school in the example above is not a very good one, you would probably help your chances of persuading people to support your campaign if your message is: 'Your school could be offering a really good education – instead X council are planning to close it – let's keep it open and work to improve it.'

Don't assume that people know very much
Most people will not be aware of the issue on which you are campaigning. You have to make them aware before they are likely to take any sort of action. So you must never assume that they know the sort of detail that you do, as committed campaigners.

Even if you are delivering leaflets round the same area or putting notices up on the board every week, there will always be people who have just moved there, people who suddenly have enough time to read the latest leaflet right through and people who have got too much on their minds to remember what you were saying last time.

So *explain as you go along*. Put in brief explanations, no more than a few words long, of almost anything that is not definitely common knowledge.

To see how this can be done, look at a newspaper – one that you do not read every day. In most cases, you'll find that you can understand an article even if this is the first time you have heard about the issue. Here is an example, taken from the *Newcastle Journal* of 6 February 1990. It's headed 'Disabled Transport Scheme in Crisis' and it starts off:

> An innovative voucher scheme to encourage disabled people to use taxis has flopped after just one year.
>
> The 'Care Cab' scheme – part of the £1m Care Services Scheme to help the disabled travel – has been boycotted by some taxi drivers who are demanding £3 minimum fares to carry wheelchair-bound and other disabled people.
>
> Their move has been described as 'disappointing' and 'surprising' by leading councillors on Tyne and Wear's Passenger Transport Authority – which will today launch a '£40,000 campaign to boost the scheme.

The rest of the article explains how the scheme works, what has gone wrong with it, and what the Passenger Transport Authority intend to do about it. It quotes several people, explaining each time who they are. So Councillor Richard Tate is 'Chairman of the PTA's general purposes committee' and Mr Dave Howard is 'The Passenger Transport Executive's Director General.'

The journalist does not need to explain where Tyne and Wear is, since it's the area the readers live in. But if it was a report in a national paper, you'd expect to see also some words about 'in the North-East of England.'

Keep away from jargon

Avoid using any shorthand terms you use outside your group, or terms with a special meaning, or sets of initials that non-experts won't know.

If you mention a report, or a clause of an Act or a Regulation, or a set of initials, always explain them. So, for instance:

- The 'Griffiths proposals' might be explained as 'The Government's proposal that local councils should buy in care and accommodation for people who are unable to look after themselves, rather than providing it directly.'
- A 'Section 115 notice' could be explained as 'a notice by the Chief Finance Officer that the council will have to stop spending money, until it has found ways to balance its budget.'
- 'LMS' could be explained as 'The new arrangements under which each group of school governors is given a fixed budget each year

to spend on the school, rather than the local council taking the detailed decisions.'

If you refer to the topic again, within a few lines or sentences, you should be safe to use the shorthand term. But if there's much of a gap, put in the explanation again. In a newsletter, people won't read every article. In a long speech, people will not be paying attention all the time, so again you need to repeat the explanation, perhaps using slightly different words.

Keep it simple

Make it as easy as possible for people to understand your message. Simple language is easier for people to take in than complicated words and sentences. Journalists in the popular newspapers are trained to write using short words wherever possible, and short simple sentences. Their editors know that many of their readers will be looking at the paper during a ten-minute teabreak or on the bus on the way to work, with many distractions and not much concentration.

You don't need to imitate their attitudes or policies in order to follow their rules of simplicity. They clearly do work – these people have millions of readers.

Many people do not read very much other than a daily paper, and perhaps a magazine. So they are used to the words we use in *talking*, and will have to stop and think if you use complicated and unusual ones. The structure of most spoken sentences is simpler than the structure of most written ones. If it is not, the listener will be lost by the end. So if you want people to grasp what you are saying easily, without having to work at it, use the words and rhythms of everyday speech wherever you can.

There's nothing patronising about this. Writing in a clear simple style takes skill and perseverance – far more so than writing in a complicated way so that only you know what you mean.

Even if you are writing for a highly educated audience, try still to keep your style simple. After all, even university professors are not on duty all the time. They could be reading your leaflet or newsletter while drinking their coffee in the staff room. Their minds will be on other things, and they won't bother to struggle to work out your meaning.

Try to follow the guidelines listed in the box.

Keep the words down

Keep down the number of words on a page, or in a speech or discussion, to the fewest that will get across the message effectively. Messages that 'go on and on' just bore people, and if they are bored they are not taking in the argument. Think of the bore who props up the bar in the local pub, or traps you at a party, for instance. Five minutes after you have

Guidelines for Writing

- Use everyday words, that your readers or listeners will know easily, rather than ones that are uncommon.
- Make every word count. Look at each one and see whether it adds anything to the sentence. Cut out the padding ruthlessly. For example, you can use 'in fact' rather than 'in point of fact'. But does either phrase make the point clearer? If not, cut it out. Another example is 'obviously'. If it is obvious, why say it?
- Search for short words to use instead of long ones. For example, use 'place' or 'area' rather than 'locality'; 'even so' rather than 'nevertheless'.
- Keep your sentences short and simple. Try to give each one a subject, a verb and an object, so that they flow through and people can see what you are getting at.
- Make your sentences *active* rather than passive – 'the child saw the dog,' rather than 'the dog was seen by the child.'
- Split your sentences rather than creating complicated ones. For example, say, 'The child was running across the road. Then she saw the dog' rather than, 'The child, after running across the road, saw the dog.'
- Spell things out. Don't try to be clever or subtle, unless you are *sure* your readers or hearers will understand the point. For example, say, 'We are still waiting to hear Councillor Jones' answer to our accusation,' rather than, 'It remains to be seen how Councillor Jones deals with the knotty problem of justifying himself.'

managed to escape him or her, the chances are that you will not remember anything you heard.

Keep your *design* straightforward and easy on the eye. Use a few images and styles well, rather than a lot in a confused way. Look at Chapters 8 and 9 for detailed ideas on this.

Make it easy

If you want people to do something, make it easy for them. Give them the exact address to write to, or tell them who to phone, or who to write cheques out to. Design forms which are easy to fill in, and make positive answers easier to give than negative ones.

If you want money from people, for instance, put down actual amounts that they can tick, rather than leave them to think about what they can afford.

Tell people who you are

People always want to know what group they are listening to or reading about. Where are they based? Who are they? If they don't know this they can become suspicious and afraid that someone is pulling a fast one on them.

So *always* include the name of the organisation, and try to give the name of an individual as well. Give a brief explanation of what the group is, if it is not obvious from its name.

> For example, Leafields Factory Campaign puts on all its literature: 'A group of local workers and residents campaigning for Leafields Factory to stay open and to be expanded.'

Use your opportunities

Take every chance to get the new supporters, and the money, you need.

Put a form with a tick-box in every publication, and an address for people to contact. Include a phone number too, if possible. Then make sure you respond quickly and efficiently. For example:

- if there's a phone number, tell people when to phone, and make sure there is someone at the other end at those times; or
- buy or borrow an answering machine, and make sure that someone phones back within a day or two, in answer to any messages left on it;
- if you are asking people to write in, make sure that letters are collected and answered as soon as possible – preferably within a week;
- if you are asking people to come to a meeting or an office, make sure they are welcomed when they get there, and made to feel valued.

An example

To show how the style can be improved, even if the material is not very promising, here are a couple of real examples from a Labour Party newsletter. The stories themselves are not what they should be. They don't include names, or link in with particular local concerns, or provide human examples that people can relate to. Even so, changing the words can make the newsletter much more interesting and readable.

It could be much better, though. For the first story, the editor needs to:

- spell out what the improvements under discussion really are. Do 'recreational and environmental improvements' mean a new play area, tree-planting and stopping traffic racing through the streets, or just a bit more street-sweeping and efforts to keep the current recreation grounds cleaner?
- be specific about the places that are going to benefit. There might only be two council estates in the ward, so why not say, 'Milton

and Shakespeare estates,' so that residents in those areas can identify with them?

SANDYFORD NEWS

Original Version
Rosemary Collins, editor of *Sandyford News*, writes:

This is a very difficult time for your Labour-controlled City Council. They are being forced to implement policies in education, health, housing and social services of which they are highly critical. Additionally they are being obliged to implement the Poll Tax, to which they have strong objections. Nevertheless, a number of recreational and environmental improvements and a schedule of housing repairs are in the pipeline for several parts of the ward. Details should be firmed up shortly and will appear in April's Newsletter.

Rewritten version
Sandyford should have brighter streets, improved recreation areas and better-maintained council houses by the end of the year, thanks to the City Council.

The Council is setting its budget at present, and discussing plans for a repairs programme for the housing estates, improvements to the recreation areas, and work to give residents a better environment to live in. The Council will announce the details very shortly, and we'll carry a full list in the next *Sandyford News*.

The Labour Party would like to do a great deal more for the area. But though the Council itself is run by Labour, we have a Conservative Government in Whitehall. They are forcing us instead to spend money on things we do not want to do, in health, social services, and housing especially. And they have made us bring in the Poll Tax, which we dislike just as much as the general public do.

Rosemary Collins
Editor, *Sandyford News*

In the second story, the editor could give an example of the type of person who could apply to pay Poll Tax once a week or fortnight. This might be, 'Mr J, a pensioner who has got just enough money in the bank to stop him claiming Income Support,' or, 'Sarah, a lone parent struggling to get by on a low wage.'

'Contact the Civic Centre,' is also very vague and rather daunting. The newsletter should say which section to contact, how (by phone or by post?) and any information people need to have with them, like their Poll Tax number.

Original version

Your Poll Tax demand will shortly be posted to you. You will automatically be offered the option of paying it in ten instalments. If you are managing on a very low income, however, you may find it easier to make weekly or fortnightly payments.

The Council is not encouraging this method of payment except for groups of people who have already been identified as suffering particular hardship. If widely used, it could be administratively costly enough to actually increase *next* year's poll tax.

If, though, you really feel that your circumstances are going to make it impossible for you to pay regularly in any other way you should contact the Civic Centre and explain your circumstances.

If you have further difficulties regarding payment do not hesitate to contact your councillors.

Rewritten version

Do you know that you can pay your Poll Tax weekly or monthly, if you're on a low income and would find it difficult to manage any other way?

The Civic Centre can arrange this for anyone in serious hardship. But they are hoping that most people take up the option to pay in ten instalments. That's given automatically when the Poll Tax demand is sent out. If too many people want to pay more frequently than that, it will cause administrative headaches. The extra cost might even mean a bigger bill for next year's Poll Tax.

If you're in hardship, contact the Civic Centre about paying weekly or fortnightly. If there are any other problems about paying, do please get in touch with one of the Sandyford councillors. Their addresses are on the back of *Sandyford News*

4

Different methods

Efficiency and effectiveness

Chapter 2 looked at the various audiences you are trying to reach, and Chapter 3 at the ways to communicate effectively. This Chapter covers the various *methods* – spoken, written, visual – that you can use. Different methods work at different times and places. Whenever you are planning publicity work, you need to think about the most *efficient*, *effective* and *practical* methods for your group.

Efficiency in this case means reaching as high a proportion as possible of the people you want to reach, and wasting the least effort in delivering the message to those you have no need to reach.

Effectiveness means giving your message the biggest chance of achieving your aim, of convincing the people concerned and persuading them to take the action you want.

Being *practical* means staying within your limits of time, money and skills, so that you can do what you set out to do well, rather than trying to do something ambitious and doing it badly.

Remember that:

- Your efficiency is only as good as your distribution system. If your letter or leaflet is carefully written for just the people who you need to influence, but is delivered to the wrong people because your mailing list is out of date or incorrect, you've wasted your effort.

- Your effectiveness is only as good as your ability to get your message across. Your leaflet could get to just the right people, and include arguments that ought to convince them, but be badly written or boring so that they don't get beyond the first paragraph. Then again your effort is wasted.

- If you want people to take a particular action, such as writing to their MP or becoming members of your group, you need to use a method that is likely to encourage this.

- Your efficiency and your effectiveness will both be improved if you can find a way of getting feedback from your audience, that is, some idea of of what they think of what you are saying, whether the

27

message is being understood correctly, or needs altering to make it clearer.

Below is a list of some of the possible methods of getting your message over to people:

- Face to face discussion.
- Phone calls.
- Individually written letters.
- Leaflets, hand addressed and delivered.
- General leaflets handed out in public.
- Posters.
- Public meetings and conferences.
- Other public events, such as demonstrations and rallies.
- Newsletters distributed to a particular group.
- Pamphlets, reports, books.
- Advertisements in newspapers and magazines.
- News stories and features in newspapers and magazines.
- Radio phone ins.
- Radio interviews.
- TV interviews.
- TV news stories and features.
- Videos, films and tape slide shows.

In the rest of this Chapter, the advantages and disadvantages of these various methods are looked at briefly, in order to help you judge which ones are most suitable.

Face to face discussion

This means talking to just one person or a small group.

For: means a 'personal touch' and you can speak to just the right people, put over the arguments that are most effective for them, make sure that they have understood each point before moving on to the next; can see immediately what impact you are having; can organise it so that people can take action – such as signing a petition – on the spot.

Against: time consuming; only possible with small audience, or with larger audience where you have enough people to divide up the work; difficult to say the same thing each time.

Other points: works best when talking to people who already know you, or at least know of you; strangers may be suspicious or hostile, or simply refuse to open their doors or stop in the street; but if the issue already has popular appeal, setting up a stall and stopping people yourselves can be highly effective.

Phone calls to potential supporters or others

For: can speak to right people, put over arguments effectively, check that they have been understood; can cover people living in a wide geographical area, whom you could not hope to see personally; can get feedback on their responses; can cover quite a large number of people if you use a 'telephone tree' (explained on page 69).

Against: can't see how audience are reacting, or get them to take action immediately; a lot of people are hostile to 'telephone selling' and this feeling of irritation is probably growing rather than reducing; some people don't like talking on the phone to strangers; many people don't have a phone, especially older and poorer people; time consuming and difficult to give the same message to everyone; could cost a lot.

Other points: again, most useful where you already know the person you are contacting, and where the message is fairly simple and you do not have to 'sell' something hard. People need some training if they are to come over well.

Individual letters

These may be handwritten, typed or computer processed.

For: makes people feel they are being contacted personally; can put over arguments consistently and at length, since they can study them at their leisure; can stress points of most importance to each individual; people can take action immediately by filling in form or sending cheque; can keep accurate record of responses.

Against: needs a lot of labour in writing or typing letters, or a lot of technology (computers and good printers) in producing them; mailing lists need to be accurate and kept up to date; could be counterproductive if letters go to wrong people.

Other points: works well for appeals for money or for something specific; needs care and skill to make it interesting; you can develop quite detailed arguments; but 'junk mail' coming through our letterboxes is devaluing these letters unless they look *very* personal; helps if the letters are signed by someone whom the recipients know, or at least know of.

Leaflets, personally addressed and hand-delivered

For: can look fairly personal, without taking too much effort; can be combined successfully with visits or phone calls; can grab attention and get across brief message clearly; can target group of people, or small geographical area; can include pictures and charts; can be designed to take action and help feedback, for instance by asking people to fill in forms.

Against: have to compete with other leaflets coming through door, so have to be eye-catching; may not be read by person you are trying to reach; involves care in putting together list of addresses, and some labour in delivering leaflets.

Other points: 'expected' method of doing certain things, like giving details of a candidate in an election; can make good use of limited financial resources; can use series delivered to same people to build up awareness of issues.

Leaflet handed out in public or delivered round streets

For: can reach large numbers of people quite quickly, and without needing much labour; can get over brief message well; can make immediate impact on people; can be used to get action, though likely to need reinforcement by other means.

Against: may not reach target groups, while reaching many others who are not target group; can annoy people; many get thrown away unread; have to compete with much other literature; difficult to get much feedback; only small amount of information can be included.

Other points: can help the chances of reaching your target audience by planning where you will hand out or deliver them; must assume people will not have seen previous leaflets, or know about issue; can be expensive if you have to print large numbers many of which are not read.

Posters

For: eye-catching and can force themselves on people's attention; will be read by people while doing other things (like queuing for the bus); can make quick point humorously or very strongly; asking people to put up poster is way of getting them to commit themselves.

Against: can get over only a very brief message; competing with commercial advertising, so need to be of a good standard; may have difficulty finding sites; may find them torn down or defaced; difficult to get action or feedback.

Other points: Good for making people aware of the issue, and then following it up by other means, such as leaflet or personal contact; helpful for telling people *where* and *when* something is happening, like a public meeting or event; can make impact in a controversy if large numbers of people show their support or opposition in this way.

Public meetings and conferences

For: can be means of putting pressure on those you want to influence; allows people to hear about the issues, ask questions, and give their views; can get public figures to commit themselves to campaign and take action; can give 'vehicle' for campaigning and publicity work both before and afterwards; can ensure feedback fairly easily.

Against: can be counter-productive if sets up hostility in those you want to influence; only a small minority of people ever goes to a public meeting; except with a controversial local issue, it's likely to be the already converted; can be very boring and give people a poor image of the organisation; potential for bad publicity if ill-attended or something goes wrong; time-consuming to organise properly and make most of publicity value; people may feel they have taken required action simply by attending; expensive to set up.

Other points: will *only* work if there is publicity work round it; in controversial issues where feelings are running high locally, can provide impressive show of support or opposition; with good speakers, even those who already know the subject can learn something new; also useful for 'limited' group such as school parents, where there is a good chance of getting a substantial proportion of the audience along.

Note: Only the publicity and public relations aspects of meetings and other public events are covered in this book; for details of how to set one up and run it, look at *Organising Things*, Pluto Press 1983, and *A-Z of Meetings*, Pluto Press 1984, and other books listed in Appendix 1: Booklist.

Other public events

This includes demonstrations and rallies.

For: can get particular message across, and do it in way that is enjoyable and makes people think well of the organisation; useful if campaign depends on getting people to feel or see something; allows people to commit themselves to supporting the group; lots of scope for publicity work round it; can be as large or small as you want; can create image for organisation very quickly.

Against: time consuming and expensive to do properly; scope for bad image and bad publicity if things go wrong; poor attendance could harm your publicity and your morale, unless well-handled with the media; may be counter-productive if you stop people doing something they want to do; difficult to get people to take further action as they will feel they have 'done their bit'; may not be able to obtain detailed feedback.

Other points: good publicity before and afterwards essential; best for issues with a lot of popular appeal, or a lot of potential for people to enjoy themselves in way that reinforces message you want to give.

Newsletters, newspapers and magazines for subscribers and supporters

For: can go into issue in depth; keep supporters informed of progress and future activities; can be used to publicise stories that are then taken up elsewhere; can be sent to potential supporters to give idea of organisation; way of building group's image and reputation; can persuade supporters to take action and ask for feedback.

Against: needs serious resources to go into writing, editing and printing; once started, can be a millstone round your neck; if dull or badly produced, can harm image; may not be enough news to fill it.

Other points: useful for an organisation with long-term aims, which can build up loyal group of supporters, especially if widespread geographically; can act as 'core' for rest of publicity activities by advertising leaflets, reports, events, personalities, and briefing people with extra details and arguments to use; need care over distribution and keeping mailing list up to date; may have to sell copies at a price, which can exclude low-income groups.

Pamphlets, reports, books, magazines for the public

For: can go into issue in depth, 'set agenda' for debate or stir up controversy; can make or build group's reputation; can be used as background material for supporters and further publicity work; can be vehicle for obtaining press coverage.

Against: time-consuming and expensive; needs planning and research; *must* be accurate; will only be read by fairly small number; unlikely to persuade people to take action unless reinforced by some other publicity; difficult to obtain feedback.

Other points: useful or essential as foundation stone of campaign, to be used as background material. Not required where issues are simple and short term, but most groups have to produce something like this as an Annual Report, and it makes sense to use it fully; distribution important.

Advertisements

For: under your control; can target it at right audience, with research; can persuade people to take action.

Against: expensive, especially TV and radio; readers may not look closely at advert or take it in; response rate may be low; difficult to get feedback; people may not believe what they see in an advert anyway; restrictions on what you can say, especially on television; will make people believe you have a lot of money to spend.

Other points: useful if announcing an event, especially in local papers, or publicising something you have to sell; proper follow-up essential, or your credibility will suffer; can be used to counter other side's propaganda, for instance during an industrial dispute.

News stories and features in newspapers and magazines

For: wide readership; can reach target audience you cannot reach any other way; no immediate financial cost (though time and effort); can get action if message powerful enough, but may not be precisely what you want; can get feedback, though perhaps from activists rather than representative section of population.

Against: *not* under your control; can be wasteful if in wrong place, or counter-productive if message is not what you want; stories need to be 'newsworthy' in editor's eyes, rather than your own; can use up a lot of time and energy; stories forgotten a few days later.

Other points: the more you know how the system works, the more likely you are to avoid distortion; can create your own 'newsworthiness'; needs careful selection of media if effort is not to be wasted; need to develop skills in writing press releases and to build up contacts

Letters to newspapers and magazines

For: you (almost) control what you say – though they might be cut; people read letters page closely, so can reach your audience well; can create 'climate of opinion' and debate with opponents; can go into detail; cheap; can get action by appealing to readers to do something specific.

Against: can be misrepresented if wrongly edited; can end up boring the readers; opponents may be seen as winning the argument if they are better at letter-writing; feedback certainly, but perhaps not from typical members of population.

Other points: useful for telling people you exist, drawing attention to issue or event, asking people to write somewhere or come to event; also for making punchy comment in debate; can organise groups of individuals to write *different* letters making the various points; may be only way a 'difficult' group, or one that's seen as not newsworthy, can get its point across to a wider audience; other media people read letters pages, and you may be contacted by local radio or TV after a letter appears in the local papers.

Radio phone-ins

For: quite large audiences, though may not be right target group; opportunity to put your argument across in a debate; can be highly effective if practised and skilful.

Against: some presenters hostile; audience may be listening with only half an ear; danger that someone more effective will have last word.

Other points: useful for hammering away at one or two major points, rather than going into detail; can organise group of individuals to phone in and create climate of opinion; could be wasteful unless your target audience listens to that programme; some local phone-ins are very influential.

Radio and TV interviews

For: big audiences, quite mixed, often including policy-makers, so can have direct influence; can debate directly with opponents; can get points across in punchy, vivid way.

Against: some presenters hostile; people not paying much attention, so overall image is what comes across; opponents may do better than you; nervous people come across badly.

Other points: training and practice important; need to know your stuff and develop your confidence; good way of getting your side of an argument across; can re-use material by turning it into news story or article; TV does not lend itself to developing complex ideas, so need to keep to two or three main points.

Radio and TV news stories or features

For: big audiences; makes impact, if not for very long, and can influence policy makers; can get action if message sufficiently strong; feedback available, but will largely concentrate on appearance and image, rather than style.

Against: depends on programme makers' priorities rather than yours; can distort your message for sake of creating good pictures; very short 'sound-bites' and 'human interest' stories rather than details of arguments; can take up enormous amount of time and have disappointing results; difficult to come across as genuine; can ruin group's image and reputation if it comes across badly.

Other points: need to know your own priorities so they do not get distorted; important to have training, practice and confidence; good for getting over punchy message but back-up detail will have to be given elsewhere.

Video, films, tape slide shows

For: can get across message clearly, with voice and pictures reinforcing each other; same message goes to every audience; can put message in vivid way that hits home.

Against: expensive to create (especially video); competing against TV and cinema productions, so people used to high standard; distribution problems; people's attention span is short, so detail that can be given is limited; difficult to get action or feedback unless reinforced by other methods.

Other points: good where you have 'captive audiences' such as branch meetings, or local organisers willing to set up meetings; to make full impact, needs written material and discussion to reinforce the message and fill in the details; cheap if you can get permission to use a video of a programme that's being made about you by professionals.

Promotional items

These may include balloons, beer mats, balloons, T-shirts, carrier bags etc.

For: can get across brief message and image of group; buying them can make people feel committed; wearing or carrying them shows the world they are committed; can add some fun to your message; way of building your image with people; can create 'climate of opinion.'

Against: can only get across very little, no subtlety in it; your message may not lend itself to humour or a clever line; high cost, much of it wasted as people wear or carry items once, then take them home and leave them in drawer; for controversial issues, people may be nervous of showing support in public; may create the impression your group is frivolous.

Other points: useful if there's wide understanding of the issues already, and you want people to show which side they are on; needs plenty of back-up from other items if they are to have an effect; budget, design and distribution all need to be planned with care.

5

Planning a strategy: points to consider

Planning your work ahead will help to:

- Make the best use of your limited resources of time and money.
- Build up your campaign through various stages.
- Reinforce your message by using different methods at different times.
- Give a consistent impression to those you want to reach with your message.

The next chapter looks at the nuts and bolts of drawing up a communications plan. This one considers more general points.

How far ahead should you plan?

Some groups hope they will have a limited life, leading up to a big event or a point where their campaign will either have succeeded or failed. For them, the publicity plan should run up to that date, or a little beyond. It could be worth doing the planning backwards – starting with the event itself and working back from that, to ensure that you can fit everything in.

Other groups, like trade unions and tenants' associations, have a continuing life. A year ahead is probably about the right planning period for you. It will see you through both the peak periods of activity and the slack ones, and take in all the actions you *have* to take anyway, like issuing an Annual Report and holding a Christmas raffle. When you have particular events, or the launches of new projects coming up, draw up a sub-plan for this and work backwards from the key date.

There are examples of worksheets to help you with this on pages 51–7.

A group that is in a crisis needs to plan too, over the short term. The essential points will be to allocate people to specific tasks, to decide on policy about talking or not talking to the media, and what you will say.

Making use of your plan

The idea is to use your plan as a working document throughout the period it covers. Check at each meeting what is to be done next, and lay firm plans for what is coming soon, and more tentative ones for perhaps two months further on. Revise the plans as you go along and as circumstances change.

Try to arrange your work so that, by the time you come to the end of your planning period, the next plan has been drafted. For instance, you could take up time at the two committee meetings before the plan runs out: one to work on the first draft, and the second to finalise it, having thought about it and done any necessary homework.

If your group has a definite goal in view, plan how you'll respond either to success or failure of your aims. Either way, you should issue a news release, respond to media contacts, and send thank you letters to supporters. If you have succeeded, you may then be able to shut up shop. If you've failed, you may want to continue the campaign in a different way. So however optimistic you are, at least sketch out what you will do after your big event. You can fill in the details once you know what the result of your work has been.

Learn from your experience

As part of the process of writing each plan, make the time to review the last one. Ask yourselves:

- What went right?
- What went wrong?
- Did we have any successes that we did not expect?
- Did we have any disasters?
- Did we keep to the budget?
- Did we keep to the deadlines and target dates we set ourselves?
- What could we have done better?
- What lessons can we learn?

Then take account of the answers to these questions as you plan the next stage.

Your failure may have been because of over-optimism in the original plans about the amount you could do, the money you could raise and the length of time you needed to carry tasks through. This is a good fault, because it shows that you are enthusiastic, and ready to push yourselves, but next time round, try to reduce your ambitions to what is feasible.

Where to start

To make the best use of your resources, build your plans around the things you have to do anyway. For example, most groups have to hold an Annual General Meeting, elect a new committee, and perhaps ask members to renew their subscriptions. You could decide to spend extra time and money on writing and designing the Annual Report and then use it throughout the year as a publicity brochure. At the time of the AGM itself you could send the report to the newspapers with a news release and get publicity even if no reporters come to the meeting.

You could use the AGM itself as a showplace for the group's work, with an exhibition of photos or some carefully prepared speeches about the activities, and plenty of publicity material about the organisation or the issue scattered around the hall.

In the same way, your letters asking people to renew their subscriptions can be used as an opportunity to involve existing members in the organisation more. You can, for instance, tell them what is happening in the group and what you'd like them to do. This might mean raising their subscription to a higher level, giving a donation, enrolling another member, or volunteering to spend some time in the office

Fundraising events can be used to produce far more than just money! More people come to the average jumble sale than to the average public meeting, so it is an opportunity not to be missed. Even a group specialising in quite a narrow subject could pick up a supporter or two. Any group like a residents' association or a schools campaign is almost certain to have some potential members among those who give jumble and come to the sale themselves. But they need to know what the issues are. So you could hand out leaflets, with a membership form on the bottom.

Plan how you can use the opportunities created by other people, too. If your group has a speaker at a meeting some other group has set up, you could offer to supply a copy of the speech so that it can go out with the main news release. If there is a photographer coming to a festival where you have a stall, arrange for him or her to take a picture of you.

You may also be able to share the cost of publicity with other groups in a way that does not reduce the impact of your work or theirs. You could, for instance, ask another group to put one of your leaflets in their next mailing, or an advertisement in their magazine, and do the same for them later.

Develop the message

Plan your publicity work so that you repeat and develop the same message several times over the weeks and months in different ways, and with different publicity methods.

This is important because people quickly forget what you have said, or perhaps only half hear it to start with. As you move through the stages of a planned campaign, the main message may alter: from simply telling them the facts, you'll move on to telling them what to do about it, and then how it can be done. But jog their memories about what the issue itself is at every opportunity.

One form of publicity can do this for another. For example, you could put a leaflet through people's letter-boxes, and also get some lapel stickers printed. Then when people see the stickers, they should think, 'Oh yes, that's the group that sent me the leaflet,' and when they see the leaflet, they will think, 'Oh yes, that's the group that has the stickers.'

Different types of publicity speak in different tones. A poster shouts at you; a leaflet can do so too, or it can talk quietly and reasonably, depending on how it is designed. Alter your tone for different purposes. Shouting is for a quick urgent message; a lower tone is for getting over the background facts.

Who is going to do the work?

A good publicity strategy is time-consuming, and involves you either developing skills or finding people who already have them. Try not to load too much on to a few people, as you will use up their enthusiasm.

You're not going to know what hidden talents you have got unless you ask. Very few people put themselves forward unless asked, in case they get rebuffed. There are many women without paid jobs or with part-time jobs well below their abilities because they are looking after children. They could be quite diffident about all the things they can do until someone approaches them.

Other people may not be confident enough to design a leaflet or a poster, but would be happy to cycle round town delivering letters to save the cost of postage, or to put leaflets through doors.

When you have a quiet patch, give people a chance to learn new skills and to build up their confidence. In a crisis, though, it is wiser to give tasks like keeping in touch with the media to the most experienced people and channel as much as possible to them, so that those dealing with the crisis or the work of the organisation can get on with it without too much distraction.

If there are not many people to get involved, then either cut your planned workload or look for more help. Don't try to overstretch yourselves, or you will simply do everything badly.

If your group makes a policy of rotating jobs among its members, put together an information pack for the main ones, explaining what each entails and giving lists of main contacts, such as local reporters and printers. Include a list of key members and their phone numbers, with a note of whether or not they can be contacted during the daytime. There are explanations of what the various tasks are in other chapters.

Looking outside the group

There may also be people outside your organisation on whom you could call for free or cheap help occasionally. This could be drawing pictures for a poster or helping you to keep up to date with research on your subject.

Start with your friends or colleagues at work. They are quite likely to share your ideas and feelings and to trust you not to get them into anything odd. Alternatively, try:

- the local Council of Voluntary Service. Some of these keep registers of volunteers, or have a full-time volunteer organiser; most will be well-informed about useful people in the area;
- community workers or people running a local community centre;
- local trade union branches;
- lecturers or students' unions at the local university, college or polytechnic. The lecturers on particular courses might be able to provide skills or advice relating to them. Someone teaching a graphic design course, for instance, might be willing to arrange for a couple of students to do some graphics for you.

Look in *Organising Things* for more ideas about who to approach, and how to go about it.

Don't overload these helpers. But if someone seems keen, ask if they would like to become more involved.

When you have to pay for work, don't try too hard to get it at a cut rate. The quality and delivery may suffer if you do. The person just will not give the same priority to you as to full-fee clients.

Making sure your help meets your needs

Any offer of help should be welcomed, but it may not be exactly what you need. The person's ideas may be too grand, or they may be suggesting something that will not fit in with the message you are trying to convey.

Try then to turn the offer round so that the group can get something it needs from that person, rather than turn them down altogether. Doing that would leave people with a feeling of being rejected, and would give the wrong impression of the group. For example:

Edgartown Disablement Action Group is composed of people with disabilities. They have already decided that they want to get across the message that they are active, independent and not to be patronised. So they need to design their activities to imply this all the way through.

When they hold their Annual General Meeting, or are seeing reporters or councillors, they will want to put someone with disabilities to the fore. They explain this to the able-bodied people who offer them help, and ask if instead they will do the fetching and carrying beforehand, and supply the refreshments at meetings, leaving the people with disabilities to do the rest.

Be fair to your volunteers

Put yourself in the shoes of someone taking on a new role in your group, or coming to do something specific for it. This person needs to know what they are doing, how they go about it, and who they are doing it for. If instead they find themselves in the middle of a battle about 'who authorised this' and 'this doesn't fit in with the decision we took last Thursday,' they will be fed up. They won't do any more work for you, and they might also tell other people what an ungrateful lot you are.

So draw up a specific 'job description' each time someone comes to help you. This could be simply a letter, or a note in the minutes. It should spell out:

- what is required;
- when by;
- who has the power to decide whether or not to use the work, or what changes to make.

So, for example, you should say whether a poster or leaflet design is to be done from start to finish by the person concerned, or is to be brought along to a committee in rough form for them to accept, reject, or fiddle about with. The size of any budget should be given, and procedure for obtaining approval of spending or overspending. For example:

Leafields Factory Campaign decide to issue a news release about the leaflet they have just delivered around the area. They ask Mary, an outside person who has expressed an interest in helping them, to do this. The minutes say, 'It was agreed that Mary should issue a news release to all the local papers, giving details of what our leaflet said, and of the story behind it. She should check the final wording of the news release over the phone with the Secretary. Any media queries would be dealt with by Mary, or by the Secretary if she was not available. The group will repay Mary the cost of any phone calls she makes, and of postage, up to £5.'

Money

Any publicity campaign involves *some* spending, if only for stamps and phone calls. Members of the group may be willing to carry some of the cost themselves. But this is unfair on those who can't afford to. You're really saying that people can only be activists if they have some cash.

Draw up a publicity budget, and ask those doing the work to claim back what they spend. If they don't feel they want to do that, they should still work out what the cost is, claim, and then give the money back as a donation. That way, the group will not be lulled into a false sense of security about the real cost. Hopefully, what you spend will be repaid by increased membership, extra grants, or success in your campaign.

As you work out what activities to undertake, put a rough price beside each one. For instance, if you're planning to send out letters to 100 people, you can guess that each one will cost you 10p to photocopy and 18p to post. So that means £28 for that exercise, plus a margin of perhaps £5 for the wasted paper and the chance that postal costs will rise. If you plan to print your Annual Report this year and circulate it to leading local people, ring up a printer and ask for a very rough quote, or look at *Print* by Jonathan Zeitlyn (see Appendix 1: Booklist for details). Then add on half as much again for postage, envelopes, and the chance of things going wrong.

Add in the cost of follow-up work. For instance, if you send out an appeal for money to your members, take account of the cost of processing the donations and sending receipts.

Then look at the group's overall budget and see how these costs can be met. Is the amount allocated for 'postage' for example, sufficient to cover the number of letters and news releases you're going to send out? If not, either cut back on your plans or persuade the Treasurer to switch cash from something else.

In future years, when planning the annual budget, take account of the costs the group is going to incur by doing active publicity work. Any grant application should include realistic figures for this. If you are aiming to be self-supporting by charging fees or bidding for contracts, include figures for publicity in your overheads.

You may be able to obtain sponsorship or donations for some items. This means that sponsors pay you a specific amount, and in return you agree to make it plain that your material is being produced with help from them. Local businesses or trade unions could be approached to sponsor your annual report, for instance. They would then pay some or all of the printing costs in return for putting their logo on the front or back. It is good advertising for them, and makes them look like a caring organisation.

ActionMatch (see Appendix 2: Addresses) specialises in finding sponsors and in training groups in how to go about finding their own. Its teaching material gives a number of hints about what type of sponsor to seek out, and how much to ask for.

Some of your publicity work can itself involve fund-raising. For instance, you can include a form asking for donations in your leaflets and newsletters, and you can hold a collection at any public meeting or conference.

With certain things, like a research report, you can make a direct charge. You'll probably be giving away a number of copies to members and others (as explained on page 130). But once details have been in newspapers or magazines, you will receive requests for copies from other people. You can charge for these at a rate which will cover the cost of all the free ones you have sent out. If that means that you are setting quite a high price, then charge that amount to any commercial group or library, and set a lower rate for individuals and a still lower one for unwaged people.

You can use the same policy at conferences or courses: budget for a certain number of free places, perhaps some low-priced ones for people who are unwaged, and some high-priced ones for people who can afford it.

However, keeping to your overall aims must have priority. A group which is trying to attract people on Social Security to use its services, for instance, will not succeed if it sets a high membership charge, even if it also has a special cut-rate for claimants. People will look at the first figure, and be put off the group. On the other hand, if the same group held a conference at which claimants were speaking in order to get their point across to professionals like teachers and social workers, they should charge as much as for the other conferences these people will attend, otherwise the group won't be taken seriously.

In your budgeting, take account also of the fact that reporters assume that they will not be charged for copies of publications, or for admission to a conference or a show. Some make it a matter of principle: more often, they simply will not buy a publication or attend an event if they are asked to pay.

Saving costs

Don't skimp on presentation or produce something that looks shabby and amateur just to save money. But *do* save by 'targeting' your activities carefully, even if this involves a little time in research. For instance if you can't afford to send a report to each of the 650 MPs in the House of Commons, see whether instead you can establish which ones have taken an interest in your particular subject. You could look in *Vacher's Parliamentary Companion*, which should be in a reference library, and gives brief details of the committees each MP sits on, for this information. Send your report only to those 20 or 30. The others would probably only have thrown it away anyway.

Similarly, if your budget for a leaflet is tight, you could keep the print run small, and hand deliver them around the area where people are most likely to be interested in your campaign, rather than giving them out in the street on Saturday. Alternatively, since the cost of printing extra copies will not be very large, it could be worth printing *more* than you need, and using the leaflet instead of something else you were planning, such as a letter to potential supporters. If you think of this in advance, you should be able to design it so that it does both jobs well.

6
The plan

Drawing up the plan

This chapter follows through an imaginary group, the Maryhill Playscheme Association. They have run holiday playschemes for children in the poorer areas of their city for a number of years. They are now worried that they are losing support from the council and teachers, because not enough is known about what they do. So they want to make sure a lot more people find out about them, over the next year.

Their original plans for the year are:

January: grant application for next summer's money goes into the Council.

February: request for members for nominations to new Committee, and for renewing subscriptions.

March: general work on sorting out sites for next summer's playschemes, making contact, finding volunteers – but nothing public.

April: Annual Report goes out three weeks before Annual General Meeting, which is held in last week of month.

May: jumble sale to raise funds.

June: planning and organising work goes on; posters and leaflets being printed for summer schemes.

July: distributing posters and leaflets, finding volunteers, sorting out problems.

August: it's all happening – events all over the place.

September: nothing planned – we're all exhausted.

October: report to council on what's happened.

November and December: nothing planned.

The group start off by thinking about their audiences. They feel that though a lot of individual parents know about the playschemes because their children go to them, they don't have much contact with the group itself. They hear about it from their children, and from the teachers at the schools. The councillors and officers hear about the project both from the schools and from the parents, but they are unlikely to visit unless specially invited. If there was any question of cutting provision, a lot of parents would probably be very upset, but it would be difficult to mobilise them because they would be mainly people who were working and so pretty busy.

The group then think about themselves, and conclude they probably come over as well-meaning do-gooders, rather amateur in their approach. If they are going to take a higher profile, they need to make it clear that they are caring and efficient. They must also show that they can be trusted with other people's children and public money. They decide that, for a start, they must type all their letters rather than handwrite them, get a permanent phone number with an answering machine, and make sure that playscheme helpers and staff always have a label saying who they are.

They then take a look at next year's programme, to see how they can make use of what they are doing anyway. They revise it, with publicity in mind, so that it reads as follows:

January: grant application has to go in. Send out a press release about it, and a background pack with facts and figures, to contacts in newspapers and local radio. Send letter and pack to councillors highlighting our needs and what we are looking for.

February: press release about results of grant application. Letter to our members and supporters, individually addressed, telling them what has happened, asking them to renew or increase their subscriptions. Separate form asking for nominations for Committee. Follow up work – letter thanking everyone who does renew the subscription, or sends a donation, to be sent out within two weeks.

March: writing Annual Report, getting it to printers, drawing up mailing list of useful contacts who ought to be sent a copy. Draft covering letter to go with this.

April: mailing of Annual Report, with news release going out at same time. Invitation to local editors, reporters and 'worthies' to come to AGM. Phone calls to find out if they are planning to come. Another news release on day, with highlights of Chair's speech, pictures of speakers. Hall to be decorated with display of photos of last year's schemes. Some refreshments available, along with membership forms and people ready to answer questions.

May: jumble sale to raise funds – news release at same time as advert goes in paper, leaflet asking for jumble, and another leaflet asking people to come along, to be distributed in local area. All to include brief explanation of what the group is, what it does and why it needs the money. Display of photos of schemes in hall, by tea counter, and copies of Annual Report and membership forms to take away.

June: as we finalise things on each site, distribute letters to parents via the schools, saying where they are and who we are. Posters and leaflets also being drafted and printed. Stress in them the message that children can have an enjoyable time *safely* at the playscheme.

July: printing of a full list in the Council's newspaper and the local papers, so that this can be used as a poster in the libraries, community centres and advice centres. Talk to local editors about possibility of double-page spread of pictures of schemes, and local TV coverage.

August: schemes running – invite editors, reporters, worthies, people who control venues and money to one that's going well. Get photographs for future use. Double-page spread in local paper, and also slots in local news on TV and radio. One person at centre to have special press responsibility this month.

September: thank you letters to anyone who gave us coverage, and to helpers and supporters. Put together display panel of pictures from summer, for future use.

October: report to Council, with nice cover and decent printing, to go to all councillors, heads of schools and those in charge of other halls we use. Include the facts and figures. Send also to MPs, local press in letter or news release, try to get local paper to photograph us presenting it to Council (perhaps with some of the children).

November: organise Bonfire Party/Halloween/Barn dance or something similar, to thank supporters and raise funds for next summer. Invite press and Mayor, try to get a few good pictures taken.

December: get invited to a few Christmas parties or bazaars at places that we use for the scheme, take display panels and leaflets about who we are, get press invited.

This plan involves extra work for the group, but it is mainly expanding and pre-planning what they would be doing anyway. It means doing things earlier, with a higher quality design, and in larger quantities. That will have an impact on the group's budget, and therefore on the grant application.

Different members might well have gone to the various social events at the schools around Christmas, so taking the display and some leaflets – which they should keep in stock anyway – is not much of an extra burden.

The group might well have had a party in November anyway, but what they are planning now is much more ambitious. It would take considerable extra work, and be a bit of a financial risk.

There's also quite a lot of extra administration – letters and phone calls following up news releases, for instance. The group need to be sure they can cope.

Revising the plan

Now comes the hard bit. Like this group, you may well find that what you'd like to do, and what you can realistically find the time and money for, are far apart.

It is better to do a few things but do them well, than to spread the resources thinly over a wide range of things and, as a result, do them all badly. So the Maryhill group, for instance, will do better to cut out the idea of a big fund-raising event in November, rather than have it turn into a fiasco because they can't put the resources into planning for it. They need people to believe that they can organise things properly, so a failure would be very bad for their overall aims.

So, regretfully, they decide to drop this idea. Instead, they'll try to arrange with the Council to let them run a stall at one of the public firework displays, with baked potatoes and hot drinks, and publicity about the group. Then afterwards the group members will go back to someone's house for a social gathering, as a thank you for all they have done.

They are also doubtful whether they know anyone with the right computer and printer for high quality personal letters. But they can find a good typewriter and photocopying facilities, so they decide that they will send the same letter to everyone, and also a standard letter thanking those who renew their subscriptions.

They don't want to drop the idea of setting up display panels, because they think it will be a very good way of showing teachers what goes on in their schools when they are away, and also telling children what they get up to. But no one is very confident at their skills in mounting an exhibition. So they decide to talk to people in the Council's Recreation Department, to find out who mounts the displays that go into the libraries. They may be able to learn from them, or persuade them to help. As a last resort, they'll pay someone, and try to find a sponsor to cover the cost.

They then redraft their plan to take account of these changes. They also try to pin a few names down:

Who is doing what

They put *Malcolm* in charge of Annual Report process, *Eva* dealing with grant application, *Francis* to contact potential sponsors and negotiate with them, *Eric* to send out press releases and keep in contact with journalists, *Nasreen* in charge of the various mailings, *Patrick* dealing with the design and printing of the leaflets and posters, *Orla* in charge of the display boards and photos, *Kwame*, as treasurer, drawing up a budget, making sure everyone knows what it is and sticks to it, and paying the bills.

Planning worksheets and checklists

This section contains a set of worksheets to help you with planning your publicity activities. You may want to adapt them to fit your organisation. If you are working as a group at a meeting, you could find it useful to copy the worksheets onto large sheets of paper, which you can put up on the wall. Keep the worksheets once you have filled them in; they'll be useful next time you have to plan, and also help you to evaluate what you have done.

Worksheet 1: What are your plans so far?

Put down on this worksheet the various activities you have planned so far, in the normal course of events or in the run up to your 'big event'.

Planning period from .... (date) to .... (date)

Subdivided into .... (weeks, months, quarters, some other

period of time)

Time Period	What we have planned so far

(continue on more sheets as necessary)

Worksheet 2: Filling in the gaps

A. Pick out from worksheet 1 periods of time when you have not planned much (or any) publicity work to keep you in the public eye, and list them below:

Thin publicity periods

A1. _____

A2. _____

A3. _____

A4. _____

A5. _____

A6. _____

(continue on another sheet if necessary)

B. Pick out events (during the thin times or at other times) where there is more scope for publicity work than you have so far planned to do:

Events that can be exploited

B1. _____

B2. _____

B3. _____

B4. _____

B5. _____

B6. _____

(continue on another sheet if necessary)

C. Now put down some ideas for using the gaps for extra publicity work, and for making better use of the events you have planned already:

C1. _____

C2. _____

C3. _____

C4. _____

C5. _____

C6. _____

(continue on another sheet if necessary)

Now add the items you have worked out to your draft plan in worksheet 1.

Worksheet 3: Your budget and your resources

This worksheet is intended to help you to draw up a rough budget for your publicity work, and then to monitor what you actually spend. The headings are the main ones under which money is likely to be spent, but you may think of others, so spaces have been left for you to write in more.

You probably have many of these headings in your accounts already. Try to separate out, as far as you can, the publicity elements of these costs from the rest, and relate them to your plans as they stand in worksheet 1.

Financial year .... / .... (or other time period)

Heading	Last year's estimate	Last year's actual	This year's estimate	This year's actual	Differences (see notes)
Postage					
Telephone					
Printing					
reports					
leaflets					
posters					
other					
Hire of					
rooms					
Hire of					
equipment					
Travel					
expenses					
Stationery					
Subscriptions,					
books etc.					
Miscellaneous					
Other (list)					

Notes on differences _____

_____

Note: if you are planning publicity activities which are major in terms of the scale on which you normally operate, put together a rough budget for these separately at this stage. It will need revision later, but it should help to ensure that you don't overstretch your resources.

Worksheet 4: People and skills

This worksheet covers the main jobs that will need to be done, and includes a note of the chapters in which you will find an explanation of the main points of that work. Some of them may not be relevant to your organisation, or you may want people to take on more than one task each.

Jobs to be done	Who will do them
1. Contact with media (Chapter 6)	
2. Dealing with printer (Chapter 9)	
3. Coordinating newsletter (Chapter 13)	
4. Drafting and designing leaflets (Chapter 11)	
5. Designing posters (Chapter 11)	
6. Looking after display at events etc	
7. Keeping research and press cuttings up to date (Chapter 16)	
8. Keeping and circulating notes of meetings	
9. Other tasks	

Worksheet 5: Filling in gaps

Now go through the list again, and see where there are gaps where you have been unable to enter a name. Write down ways in which you can fill these. These might include sending someone on a course to learn a new skill, bringing in an outsider, or someone taking on more than one job while helping another less experienced person learn.

Gap	Ways we can fill it

(continue on more sheets as necessary)

Worksheet 6: Revised plans

This is set out in the same way as worksheet 1. It is for you to fill in after you have gone through the other worksheets, taking account of what is practical, and what you can find the money and the people to do.

Time period	Plans we now have

(continue on more sheets as necessary)

Worksheet 7: Evaluation

You may want to fill in one of these for each major activity, or for a period over which you have had several things planned. Or you may want to do your evaluation at the end of the planning cycle, before you start the next set of plans. In any event, keep these evaluation sheets, and compare them with those you fill in later. If the same problems keep on recurring, think about the reasons for this, and ways in which you can deal with them.

Event or period covered ....

What went right?
_____

What went wrong?
_____

Successes we did not expect?
_____

Why?
_____

Disasters?
_____

Why?
_____

Did we keep to the budget?
_____

Reasons for variations (up or down)
_____

Deadlines and target dates we kept
_____

Deadlines and target dates we failed to keep
_____

Reasons
_____

What could we have done better?
_____

What lessons can we learn?
_____

Date evaluation done ....

PART II
Methods of communication

7

Talking to people

This chapter covers:

- Face to face discussion.
- Talking on the phone.
- Making speeches.

Talking to people, as individuals and small groups, is one of the best ways of communication there is – and the one in which we all have the most practice. Talking to large groups is less good, because it is difficult to gauge your audience's reaction or take account of their objections. But it is still worthwhile, and worth doing well. Talking on the phone suffers from the same problems, but again can be useful. In all cases you'll help people to understand what you are saying and reinforce your message if you put your main points on a piece of paper to give them as well.

Face to face discussion

Examples of this would be.

- Having a few words with a succession of strangers, as you collect signatures for a petition, or sell campaign items, on a Saturday morning in the street.
- Speaking to people after you have knocked on their doors, to get their views on an issue or on how they will vote (usually called 'canvassing').
- Going round people in the workplace, or at a community centre or a club, to explain your arguments and ask for their support, or to collect money.
- Having a meeting with some more influential people – perhaps MPs or councillors – or a small group (usually called 'lobbying').

One of the best examples of campaigning through face to face contact was in the Political Fund Ballots, organised by trade unions in 1984. Union activists were briefed, and talked systematically to their members at the workplace, persuading them to vote in favour of continuing political funds. Leaflets and posters hammered home the message. There was a good turnout, and a high 'yes' vote in every case.

Who to talk to

Decide first of all who you are trying to reach. It might be everyone who lives in a certain area, or uses a particular club or facility, or works in one place, or is a member of your group or another one. Make, or get hold of, a list of all of them. You should not need to be devious about this. If you are, it will hamper you in your work. People like to know where you have got their address, and tend to be suspicious if you cannot tell them.

If you are going round the streets, for instance, you can buy a copy of the electoral roll from the local council. This is supposed to list everyone who has registered as a voter at each address, though it's not always accurate. If you are working through the members of a club, ask the secretary for a copy of the membership list; in many cases you will have a right to this, under the club's constitution. Divide up the list between your different helpers and tell them:

- How long they have got.
- What to say and what questions to ask.
- What information you want back.

If there's a lot to do, give it out in stages, so that it feels more manageable.

Start with the easiest targets – people you are pretty sure of anyway – and work along the line to those who are least likely to support you. By the time you reach the really hostile ones, you will have had plenty of practice in your arguments. You'll know that you are not alone in thinking as you do but that, on the contrary, they are the odd ones out. If you run out of time in your campaign, missing them out won't matter that much. For example:

In the Political Funds campaign, the advice was to start by making a list of everyone who had to be approached, and guess at what their attitudes would be. The strong supporters were talked to first, then those who were lukewarm or apathetic, and only after that the ones who were known to be hostile. By then, according to one shop steward who was involved, 'everyone was talking about the issue at the workplace. The hostile ones tended to back down, or at least keep quiet, because they felt they were going against the tide.'

Decide what you want

Work out what you hope to gain by speaking to people in this way. It might be signatures on a petition, a promise of support for later, or money for your campaign now. Then decide how you'll achieve what you want. How are you going to introduce yourselves? What should be your opening arguments, and what points should you make as back-up? What objections are going to be raised and how can you answer them?

Write down the main points of your argument and key facts as a sort of script. Practise on each other if you are nervous. Make sure you know and understand the gist of what you are saying, rather than learning the precise words. Revise your script as the campaign progresses, to keep up to date, and also to give the answers to the questions that are asked frequently.

An example

Here is an example of a script for campaigners trying to keep their local village shop and post office open:

Notes for canvassers in Village Shop Campaign

Introduce yourself. Say your name, and that you have lived in or near the village for ... years. Ask if they are busy, or are able to spend a few minutes talking. Ask if they use the village shop regularly, or at all. Make a note of their reply beside their name on your list.

Explain that it is likely to close in three months' time when Mrs Woodford retires, as the Post Office say that it is not worth keeping the sub post office going, and the shop can't survive without it. Give them a copy of the leaflet.

Say that the group has got together to try to save the shop because they feel that it is a real centre for the village, and that without it a lot of the older people, and the young families without cars, or where the husband takes the car to work, will have difficulties and a lot of extra expense. Ask what they think, and make a note of their reply.

If they say they can't see what can be done, explain that the group are getting up a petition, and also putting together a proposal for the Rural Development Commission and the County Council to subsidise the shop.

Tell them about the meeting on 29 September, and ask if they can come. Note down what they say. Ask if there will be problems with transport, and offer to arrange a lift there and back if so. Note these names down on your separate list.

At the end of your conversation, draw their attention to the address and phone number of the Secretary at the bottom of the leaflet, for them to contact with any queries. Thank them for spending time talking to you.

For anything more complicated than getting signatures in the street or rattling a collecting tin, you'll need a way of recording who you have spoken to, what their responses are, and any further points that have to be taken up. The Labour Party uses 'canvass cards' when they are asking for support in elections. Figure 7.1 is an example of one of these, which you could adapt to your own purposes.

Some people will ask questions or raise issues that take up more space than allowed on this, so each person should carry a notebook as well.

With anything you can't deal with on the spot, follow it up if possible by writing or calling back with a response. But don't make promises of action you can't carry out; if you know your resources will not allow you to follow up, say so.

After a session of talking to people in this way, those involved should try to get together and exchange notes. Make someone responsible for keeping a tally of the number of contacts made, the number of 'yes' and 'no' responses, and the numbers who didn't know or didn't care. If progress is too slow, the group will have to decide whether to drop some of its plans, or work faster.

Discuss here also the arguments that have been raised, and what people said in reply. If there's a point being made that you hadn't thought of, or if your arguments don't seem to be convincing people, this is your chance to try a different approach.

How you look

If you're going round the streets, it is best to be in pairs, preferably a man and a woman together. Dress appropriately: being too smart can be as off-putting as being too scruffy. Most often, this will mean wearing neat, conventional clothes. Otherwise, you will distract those you are talking to, since they will be looking at you rather than listening.

There are people whose appearance is against them, and who may have to decide not to undertake some work, or only do so under certain conditions. Large men, for instance, can be intimidating when knocking on front doors in the evening.

Always introduce yourselves, and offer any leaflet or piece of printed material you are giving out at the start. Look directly at the person you are talking to, and smile when you can. Looking at the ground, or away from them, will make you seem shifty. Put your points briefly, clearly and politely. Tell the other person just what you want them to do. Say where you got their name and address from if it is not obvious.

Try not to lose your temper, however much you are provoked. If you do, it is that which will be remembered, rather than your arguments. *Listen* to what the other person tells you in response. If he or she raises an objection to what you are saying, or asks for more explanation, take it seriously and give them a brief clear response. If you don't know something, say so. Watch out for signs that people are bored, or

Figure 7.1 Labour Party canvass card

Card No. _____ Ward _____ Polling District _____ Polling Station _____

DOUBTFUL	LIB/SDP	TORY	LABOUR	STREET RADLAND COURT	REMARKS	CAR	PV
				453 Thompson, Rosemary C. 2			
				453 Thompson, Christopher L. 2			
				455 Barrett, Peter, A. 4			
				456 Holmes, Alan 4			
				457 Holmes, Sandra 4			
				458 Thompson, Andrew R. 6			
				459 Hogan, Michelle G. 6			
				460 Cunningham, Andrew 8			
				461 Cunningham, Gail L. 8			
				462 Miller, Jonathon 10			
				462 Miller, Lisa A. 10			
				464 Smith, Norval B. 12			
				465 Craig, Stephen L. 12			
				466 Craig, Barbar D. 12			
				467 Watson, Stephen 14			
				468 Watson, Petra C. 14			
				469 Murray, William J. 16			
				470 Murray, Mary 16			
				471 Monaghan, Sandra C. 18			
				472 Fisher, George T. 18			
				473 Struthers, Iris 18			
			Position Register Numbers				
				Do not paste below this line			

CANVASS TOTALS   1st   LABOUR _____   2nd   LABOUR _____
                         TORY _____   TORY _____
                         LIB/SDP _____   LIB/SDP _____

Reverse of card

When an elector on this card has

MOVED OUT

Please try to secure the following information

1. Your task is to identify Labour's support from individual electors.

Poll No.	REMOVED TO	D	A	F

2. Please check that the person canvassed is the elector whose name is on the register.

3. Please check all other electors in the household.

Where a person has

MOVED INTO

one of the addresses on this card–

Please try to secure the following information:

4. Please identify the Party for those electors supporting other candidates and any who might be won over to support the Labour candidate.

NAME	House No.	REMOVED FROM	D	A	F

5. Mark your canvass card in the appropriate column.

6. If car is wanted, please note the time required.

7. If window bill has been supplied, please mark WB on card.

Any other special report

8. Where an elector is not contacted, leave a blank.

_____

_____

9. At the end of the canvass please return this card to the Committe Room.

_____

_____

_____

_____

simply feel that they have talked enough, and don't outstay your welcome. Try also to avoid being buttonholed by people who want to go on talking for ever. The time you spend with them is taken away from others whom you also want to contact.

When to do it
In a workplace, or some other centre, try to pick a time which is fairly quiet, when people are relaxed. A teabreak, or just after lunch, may be the best time. Don't wait until they are dashing to go home.

Knocking on doors in the street is best done in daylight, though in winter you will have to work in the dark – in pairs – if you are to get much done. Since many people are afraid to open their doors to strangers after dark, send people out during the day if you have anyone available. They have a chance at least of catching elderly and unemployed people.

Outside London, the majority of people are home from work about 5.30 or 6.00. In London, it is rather later. After 8.30 or 9.00, you'll be wasting your efforts because people won't answer the door.

At weekends, it's worth door-knocking on a Saturday afternoon, or a Sunday morning after about 11.00. Check if there is an important sporting event on the television – you won't be popular if you disturb it!

Making contact on the phone

This method has been widely used in the US by campaigning groups, but is only just coming into use in the UK. It works best when you are talking to people you know, or with whom your links are fairly close. You could use the phone, for instance, to contact the other members of a club or parents at a school. It can also work well if you write a letter, or distribute a leaflet, to explain in advance what the issue is and tell people that you are going to phone.

Getting hold of phone numbers can be a long task, especially if people are spread around the country, so build this into your timetable at the planning stage. It will also be expensive, now that directory enquiries are being charged for.

If you are using someone else's phone, reimburse them. Keep the cost down by ringing in the afternoon or evening, and by phoning back rather than hanging on if someone is not immediately available.

If you get an answering machine, leave a brief message saying who you are and that you will call back. If someone says they are in the middle of something, take them at their word, apologise for disturbing them, and ring off. It may in fact be a way of saying that they don't want to talk to you. But if you try to force yourself on someone's attention, they won't listen anyway.

Work out what you are going to say in advance. Write the main points on a set of index cards that you can spread out in front of you.

An example

Here is an example, taken from a fundraising appeal to the members of a school's Parent Teacher Association:

Card 1: ask if you are speaking to the person named on list. If not, ask if s/he is available or could ring back.

Card 2: introduction. Say, 'You don't know me, but my child is at the same school as yours, and I'm involved in the Parent Teacher Association. That's what I am phoning about. I got your name and number from the school secretary's list.'

Card 3: explanation. 'We are looking for funds for refurbishing the library. We need £10,000 altogether, and we're going to have a series of fund-raising events later in the year. But we need some cash to get started, and we are asking parents for donations of between £5 and £10. Can you help?'

Card 4: if favourable. Give details of how to donate, which were on leaflet sent home with children from school, which they should have seen. Offer to send one if they have mislaid it. Thank them very much and goodbye.

Card 5: if cautious or hostile. Don't try to argue, say you'll make a note of their comments and pass them on to the committee, thank them for their time in listening, and goodbye.

Behave as if you have the other person's face in front of you. Sit up straight, smile at the appropriate points, don't fiddle around with other things or start reading something while the conversation is going on. People will be able to tell if you are giving the phone call only half your attention.

Introduce yourself clearly. Keep your arguments brief, and repeat them more than once, in different ways. It is quite hard to concentrate when listening on the phone, because the message of the voice is not being reinforced by anything visual. So try to avoid complicated messages on the phone.

Keep good records of whom you have spoken to, what responses you got, and where you have left a message or are expecting to call back.

Follow up with a letter or a leaflet, if you did not send one in advance. A memory of a phone call tends to be worse than a memory of a face to face conversation, since there are no visual clues.

Telephone trees

If you plan to use the phone regularly as a way of contacting people you could spread the work by using a 'telephone tree'. To do this, arrange in advance to have one central coordinator, who starts the process, and a lot of others who will each do a small amount. The coordinator rings perhaps five other people, who each ring five more, who each ring five more, and so on. It does not take very long to contact everyone in a large group this way.

For this to work properly:

- People need to have a list of which numbers to ring, and clear instructions about what to do if they can't get hold of someone. This might mean reporting back to the coordinator, who then takes on the missing person's role, or it might mean making the extra phone calls themselves. The nearer the root of the tree the gap is, the more important it is that it is filled.

- The message has to be very brief and simple, if it is not to be distorted as it moves further along the 'tree'. Confine it simply to facts, such as when and where a meeting is to be held. Don't try to use it as a method of getting an argument across, as it is difficult to keep control of what's being said.

Talking at a meeting

Small meetings

You might want to arrange a special meeting with a small group – perhaps councillors or MPs, perhaps people specially affected by something you are proposing.

You'll have longer to deal with the subject than on the doorstep or in the workplace – perhaps half an hour, or an hour at most. But these will be busy people, with their minds on other things. The politicians are likely to think they are granting you a favour in listening to you at all. So without being servile, make it plain that you are grateful for their time, and that you do not intend to waste it.

Put together a short summary of your major points, and hand it over at the beginning of the meeting, along with any background documents that you can. Many people are unlikely to read more than the summary, but will feel reassured by the rest of the material. Spell out exactly what the facts of the issue are, as well as your arguments in favour of or against it.

It will often be useful to provide photographs or diagrams that reinforce the points you are making. Make sure your document is grammatically correct, and that there are no typing or spelling errors in it. Check also that its meaning is clear. The document could be passed on to those who are opposing you, and who are looking for any excuse to pick it to pieces and say, 'But what does it really mean?'

You might want your written material to be re-used by the people you are lobbying. For instance, you might hope that the Council officers would put your arguments in their report. Make this easy for them by arranging your material as they would. Use roughly the same style as they do, without making it too obvious. They then can lift your work completely – though they are not likely to give you credit for it.

If you are talking to people with power, you'll probably have to visit their office or meeting place, rather than them coming to you. This can put you at a disadvantage. So allow plenty of time, check out exactly where to go, and whom to ask for.

If they are coming to you, make sure your place is clean and tidy, and looks friendly and welcoming. Take down out-of-date notices, or ones that are private to members of the group. Throw out the dead plants, empty the waste-paper basket, and don't leave dirty coffee cups around.

More than one person should attend any meeting, but one individual should be the main speaker. Arrange beforehand when the others are going to join in with comments. Put together a 'running order' that tells you briefly who's going to say what, and what the main points are.

There's an example of one of these in *Organising Things* (see Appendix 1: Booklist). There's also an example of the sort of briefing to put together for this purpose.

Disagreements between you should be sorted out beforehand or afterwards – not in front of the people you are talking to. One person should take notes of what is said, and write them up so that other people can read them afterwards. You could then send a copy of the notes to the people you are lobbying, or put the main points in a letter to them.

If they have committed themselves to do something, this is one way of pinning them down. Your letter could say something like:

> I hope you consider that this is an accurate report of our meeting. If I do not hear from you, I shall assume that it is acceptable.

If you are sending out a news release about the meeting, this needs to be done very quickly afterwards, while it is still 'newsworthy'. You might even want to send it out in advance, with an embargo (explained on page 183) on it. This would mean, though, that you could only include what you said, not the response you received.

Larger meetings

Setting up a meeting of any size properly is time consuming, and the arrangements for the meeting overall will matter as much as the speeches to the impression that gets over to people. A speaker has to be very good indeed to overcome the problems of a cold draughty hall, no leaflets to take away and unfriendly stewards and supporters. Look at *Organising Things* to check details of how to set up a meeting and make the best use of it, and at *A-Z of Meetings* for ideas about procedures. This section concentrates on the speeches at the meeting, but to help your planning we have provided a checklist of other points to think about:

Meeting Checklist

Leaflets advertising the meeting.

Posters.

Press releases, in advance, on day, afterwards.

Putting information about your organisation in the hall.

Making the place look attractive.

Making sure the audience is comfortable.

Microphones.

Speakers' notes in advance.

Looking after your guest speakers.

Does platform give good impression of your organisation if someone wants to photograph it?

Invitations to press and media.

Membership leaflets available.

Leaflets and handouts on chairs.

Things for people to buy – books, badges, posters.

Refreshments.

Speeches to a large group are not a very good way of communicating. Your audience will only take in part of what you say, and very few will go away with much idea of the details. There is a place for the great 'set-piece' speech, which sends people away uplifted and determined to use all their energy in the campaign. But it's a fairly limited place, and a limited number of people can have this effect. For most people, it's a matter of doing your best to get across the important points, without boring people or losing them.

The smaller the audience, the more informal you can be. With 10 or 20 people, you can ask them questions and make the event into a discussion rather than a speech. With larger numbers, this will not work.

The larger the group, the less individual the communication is going to be, and the lower the chance of clearing up any misunderstandings.

Any first speech is bound to be a nerve-racking experience. Don't believe anyone who says they were not scared. But once you have got through it, nothing can ever be as bad again.

When working on your speech, think about who is likely to attend, and how much they will know already. Most of your audience will probably already be committed, but there will be some who know very little. So if you are the only speaker, explain the issues from scratch near the beginning of the speech. If there are several speakers, the first person should do this, and the others should explain any new issues from scratch in the same way. The organiser of the meeting should contact the speakers in advance to arrange this.

Work out a logical order for what you are going to say and stick to it. It is easier to follow a speaker whose train of thought is clear than one who dodges about from point to point, or makes a lot of side-comments. Make sure your sentences come to an end, rather than being left hanging in the air.

Draft your speech in advance. Only a few very experienced speakers talk well off the cuff. Some people like to write every word down. Others prefer to put down the main points, perhaps on small cards or separate sheets of paper. Until you have developed the skill, the best way is to combine these two methods – to start by writing out the speech word for word, work on that until you are happy, and then summarise it on cards. Try to use them only as reminders, though. Look at your audience as much as you can.

Keep your speech short. Ten or fifteen minutes is long enough for most people's concentration. Time yourself at home beforehand. Start in an upbeat way, saying who you are and why you are there; then tell people briefly what you are going to cover; then do so; then summarise what you have said, and make it plain what you are expecting them to do. When you've said what you intend, say something like, 'Thank you, Chair, for letting me speak,' and sit down.

Here is an example of the sort of summary you should put in at the beginning of a speech. It's taken from the village shop campaign used as an example on page 63:

> I've been asked to speak as someone who has involved in village life for many years. I want to talk about how the shop acts as a centre for many people, especially the older ones, and what we will lose if it closes. I also want to talk about the difficulties it will cause for people without much access to private transport.
>
> Then, before we all get depressed, I want to talk about how it could be kept open and especially about the plans we're taking to the authorities.

Those plans need support if they are to go ahead, because they will mean people in the village putting in time and money. So I shall be asking for your reactions. Then I will say what the plan of action is from now on, and leave enough time for questions and discussion at the end.

Try to keep the speech fairly light. Keep any jokes or anecdotes short, and make sure that they contribute something to the point you are making. Don't risk a joke that some members of the audience may find offensive: a protest, or booing instead of clapping, will ruin the atmosphere. Sarcasm is difficult to get across, unless it is very heavy.

Try to provide copies of a leaflet or a handout – no more than one or two pages long – giving a brief summary. Hand this out as people come into the meeting, so that they can read it while waiting for the meeting to start.

While speaking

Unless the meeting is very small, it's usually best to stand up while you are talking. It shows you respect the people you are speaking to, and your voice also carries better.

Pick out a few people at the back of the room, and address them directly. You'll then automatically project your voice in that direction, without needing to shout, and people all over the hall will hear you better. Watch for changes of expression, whether yawns or smiles. They will help you know if you are getting your points across successfully. If there are both friends and strangers in the audience, look at the strangers more than the friends. It's more important that you are communicating with them, since they won't give you the benefit of the doubt.

Don't stand too close to a microphone, because it will start to whistle.

If you get interrupted by a heckler, keep calm. Say something like, 'I was just coming to that point,' or 'Thank you for making that point,' and go on with what you were saying. Or you can simply pause, and then continue with some comment like, 'As I was saying before I was interrupted...'

Some people are very good at thinking up quick witty remarks on the spot to throw back at hecklers. It's a useful skill to have, but some of these ripostes can be hurtful or downright offensive, and can put your audience on the heckler's side. It is probably best to keep the witty replies for the pub afterwards.

If the person chairing the meeting interrupts you, perhaps to tell people to keep quiet in the audience, don't be put off your stride. Wait until he or she has finished, and then say, 'Thank you, Chair,' and get on with what you were saying.

If there's a disturbance, or you provoke clapping or laughter during your speech, stop while it is going on, and then pick up where you left off.

Answering questions

Questions are useful because they give the audience a change of voice, allow people to clarify what the speaker has said, and give the speaker the chance to reinforce the different points in a new way. Keep your answers short, clear, and to the point. Don't lose your temper even with people who are being offensive.

It's better to have a few questions after each speaker; if they all come together at the end, after all the speakers have had their turn, it's rather boring for the audience.

Either the Chair, or the speaker, should repeat the question briefly before answering it. This will help people who did not hear it properly the first time, and also give you time to think about your answer.

At the end

You may be given the chance to sum up at the end of the meeting. Use this to reinforce the points you have already made, so that people go home with them fixed in their heads. Don't bring in new arguments or facts and figures at this stage. Try to stay around at the end of the meeting to talk to people who were too shy to ask questions in public or to people who want to declare their support and offer help. Take a note of potential supporters' addresses. Someone should then follow up as soon as they can, while the enthusiasm is still burning.

8
The printed word

This chapter covers the points to think about when arranging to produce any sort of printed matter, such as:

- Leaflets.
- Posters.
- Newsletters.
- Pamphlets, longer reports and books.
- Letters to supporters or potential supporters.

The next Chapter covers getting things printed. Chapters 11–14 then look at points about the specific types of printed material. Look back also at Chapter 4 to remind yourself about the basic rules for all communication.

Planning

If your material is going to look good, be easy to read, and get into the hands of the right people at the right time, you need to plan for it.

Start with a rough idea of what you are going to produce. This is important, because the same words, especially 'leaflet' and 'report', mean different things to people. One person might mean two pages, another 20. Do a rough sketch, or put together a 'dummy' to make sure everyone agrees with what you are doing and how it should look.

Work out a single sentence that describes its *purpose*, as explained on page 8, and another that says what the main point is, as explained on page 17. (If it's a newsletter or magazine, each article would need one of these sentences as well.) Give this sentence to the writer, and also the designer. Headlines, pictures and cartoons should all be planned round it, to reinforce the point you are making.

You then need to sort out:

- A budget. Even for something small, it's worth doing this. Chapter 9 explains how to get quotes from printers. Remember to include the cost of other items like artwork and postage.

- A timetable. Decide when you want the material produced by, then work backwards from that. Set a timetable and a series of deadlines, and then keep to them.

- Who is going to do what. No magic will produce a leaflet or a report: it's sheer hard slog. There are four jobs you can't do without: the editing, the writing, the design, and the distribution. These are explained in the next few pages.

There are checksheets on pages 100–3 to help you with this planning job.

The tasks involved

This is only a brief summary. Charles Foster's book, also published by Journeyman, goes into much more detail (see Appendix 1: Booklist).

- The *editor* is responsible for taking the project from the point where it is an idea in the committee's head to the printer turning up with boxes of the finished product. S/he has to sort out what's to go into it; persuade the people who are writing and designing it to get on with the job; collect it from them and get the artwork done (explained in the next chapter); get it to the printers and deal with any problems on the way through, and get it back before the deadline.

- The *writer* collects the information and writes it down in the right number of words, by the right date.

- The *designer* puts the words, and the pictures, in a form which makes them attractive and conveys what you want them to, and produces the *artwork*.

- The *distribution worker* ensures that the finished product gets out of the boxes and into the hands of those who read it, by organising people to hand it out in the street, put it through letter boxes, address and fill envelopes, or pack parcels.

One person could do everything – though unless your project is very small and simple this is a recipe for a nervous breakdown. Or each job could be shared within a team. But however you do it, you need to know who has *responsibility* for each function. If you simply make a general commitment that, 'we'll all do a bit,' nothing will happen.

You don't have to keep all these jobs within your group. You can buy in, or borrow, help from other people to cover skills you haven't got. So you could get in a designer from outside, for instance, and pay someone to put your newsletters into envelopes and post them for you.

It's then even more important for the editor and the distribution worker to coordinate what is happening.

The next few sections cover the role of the editor; after that come sections on design. The questions of what and how to write, and how to distribute the publication, are covered in the Chapters on particular types of publication in Part III.

Commissioning

'Commissioning' simply means getting people to commit themselves to write or design something. It's part of the editor's job. If you are paying for the work, then a commission creates a contract on both sides, and you will usually have to pay for it even if you don't finally print it. With volunteers, there's not a legal obligation in the same way, but you should take the process just as seriously.

When you ask someone to do a piece of work for a publication, explain:

- What subject you want it on, and the 'angle' you are asking for. If you've worked out the aims of the publication in a single sentence, as suggested above, give them this.

- How long you want it to be. Calculate it as a number of words. How many words you get on a page, or on one side of a leaflet, depends on the layout and the size of the typeface. If you can't work it out, ask your printer's advice or find something that looks similar to your planned publication, and count the words.

- When you want it by. Give a date several days before the *actual* date you need their contribution by. This gives you time to chase them up, and also to edit the work (explained below) if you need to.

- The form you want it in. Ask for it as a draft, typed if at all possible, double-spaced (that is, with a blank line between each line of text), with margins at least an inch wide all round. When you are commissioning illustrations, say whether you want to see 'roughs' first, or simply the final work.

- If you are paying, what the fee is. You should expect to follow at least the guidelines in the National Union of Journalists' *Freelance Fees Guide*. Those are minimum rates, so if you are expecting them to put in a lot of work, you should offer more. Offering a 'token fee' is an insult. It is better to ask them to donate the article or illustration because you are a good cause.

- Who the likely readers are. If you are asking for work from someone who doesn't know your organisation or your publication, send them information about it and a copy of anything similar you have already published.

Talk to the person first, whether face to face or on the phone, and then write a letter confirming all these details. Warn them that you will have to edit it, and might need to cut parts out altogether, as explained below.

Editing

This is the process of tidying up a piece so that it is ready for publication. When a piece of work (usually called 'copy') comes to the editor, s/he has to check whether the style is the same all through the piece, and if it is what's wanted. The editor may need to make changes, such as splitting up long sentences into two, or changing the order of sentences round.

S/he also needs to make it fit in with other pieces in the same publication, or other publications by your group. This will mainly be on small points, like whether you use capital letters at the beginning of certain words or not (for instance, whether you say 'Social Fund' or 'social fund'). If you produce a lot of published material, the editor should draw up a set of rules, called the 'house style' and put them all together on a 'style sheet'. Give this to the people who are doing the work.

Figure 8.1 is an example of part of one, taken from Journeyman Press's own material for authors.

Most of the editor's work is on these small, important points. But occasionally someone will misunderstand what they were asked for, or just produce something very bad. Then the editor may have to do a lot of alteration, perhaps rewriting sections completely. It may also be necessary to shorten a piece, and this could mean cutting out a sentence here and there, or taking out whole paragraphs. Appendix 1: Booklist includes books that go into detail about the skill of editing.

The editor must not make alterations that put opinions into the other person's mouth, without checking them first, or giving the piece back to the person who wrote it for them to approve. At the least, it should be discussed with them over the phone. If you are working to a very tight deadline, though, this is not always possible. The best thing then is to send them a copy of the final version afterwards, with a polite note saying why the changes were needed and why the editor could not be in touch beforehand.

If the ideas in the piece are not in line with the group's policy, then the editor will have to question whether to publish it at all. One possibility is to print it with a 'disclaimer' saying that these are the individual's personal opinions, not those of the group.

Figure 8.1

Capitals
Avoid too many capital letters – they are often unnecessary. As a rule, use initial capital letters to distinguish the specific from the general – titles, brand names, institutions, etc. Political subjects are tricky, such as State/state, party/Party – so aim for consistency, and let your editor know which approach you have adopted. We prefer 'the Labour government of 1974–9', but 'the Labour Party'. Use a capital when referring to a chapter, e.g. 'see Chapter 10'.

Commas
Omit the comma before 'and'/'or' in lists of three or more items (e.g. red, white and blue) unless the list is complicated and the commas add clarity. Commas are unnecessary preceding or following a parenthetical dash and before the opening of round brackets. Be sparing with commas: they are not needed after an opening phrase such as 'In the summer of 1939 ...' or before and after 'of course'.

Ellipses
Insert a letter space preceding and following ellipses (dots), where they indicate omitted material in a quoted passage, e.g. 'more enlightened doctors ... began to question the universality of their diagnoses.' Use 3-dot ellipses.

Apostrophes
Use 's' for the possessive case in names and surnames ending in 's' wherever possible, such as in Charles's, St Thomas's, etc. No apostrophe is used in All Souls, Earls Court, Johns Hopkins, St Albans, etc., or in plurals of capital abbreviations such as NCOs.

Hyphens
Again, the most important point is consistency. Introduce them to avoid ambiguity, such as in best-known example, or best known example, depending on the sense; deep-blue sea or deep blue sea, etc. *Hart's Rules* has a useful list of hyphenated and non-hyphenated words, and the *Oxford Writers' Dictionary* contains spelling guidelines though both are a little out of date; modern usage tends to omit the hyphen in words such as socioeconomic, macroeconomic etc.

If the editor decides not to use something at all, after asking for it to be written, s/he *must* tell the author, before the publication comes out without their piece in it, otherwise they will certainly be deeply offended.

If you have commissioned something from someone outside the group, or a member who is not directly involved in the publication, it's usually wise to arrange for someone else to read it in its original form, and comment on it. This gives the editor a second opinion if s/he wants to alter something or reject it. It also gives the group a safeguard in case the editor is allowing his or her prejudices to take over.

Another group member involved in the publication could do this. Alternatively, you might want to send a copy of the draft to an outside person, with a request for help, if it's a subject they know about and you do not. Phone and ask first if they mind you doing this, rather than just sending something unannounced through the post.

Design

This is only a brief summary. Jonathan Zeitlyn's book *Print: How You Can Do It Yourself*, also published by Journeyman, goes into much more detail (see Appendix 1: Booklist).

A good design *attracts* the people you want to attract, is *readable* by them and puts across the *image* and the *message you want*.

The design also needs to match the intended use. A leaflet that is going to be handed out in the street needs to be eye-catching, or it will be ignored or dropped unread. The design for a serious report that is being sent to experts should be much more sober, so that you are not accused of trivialising the issue.

Do a rough design first, and test it out before you go into production by asking people who are not involved to tell you what they think.

Think what skills are available to you. Chapter 9 suggests ways in which you could find help or get training. There are many books about design, and some of these are listed in the booklist. But if your group can only do the simplest form of work, then keep it simple and do it well. Alternatively, work out what you want done, and pay a professional to do the job properly, or at least some part of it.

If you are producing a long report, for instance, your budget may only run to having it duplicated. But you could smarten it up by having the covers professionally printed on stiff card, using your logo and a striking colour. Or you might be able to afford better quality printing, if you were able to make a neat job of collating, folding and stapling yourselves.

Keep any design simple and straightforward. Don't overcrowd your paper. Break the material into smaller sections, by using sub-headings or by drawing lines between different parts. This will make it easier for people to take in. With A4 paper or larger, words in two columns or more are far easier to read than long lines of print. Restrict yourself to one or two different typefaces, to keep your design uncluttered. Ring the changes instead by using bold or italic versions, or different sizes of the same type.

Pictures and graphics

Include pictures, cartoons or diagrams where they will make it easier to get the message across, but not otherwise. A simple decorative border around an announcement in a newsletter, for instance, will draw attention to the announcement. But one that is too complicated will draw attention *away* from the words and towards itself.

Link the pictures with the message. If, for instance, you are saying that a club is open to everyone and there are activities for men and women, check that your pictures do include both men and women.

You can obtain pictures by drawing them yourself, tracing them from other publications, using dry transfer lettering (like Letraset and other brands) or photocopying them from one of the special books of graphic design that are available. For instance, Journeyman Press publish a book of copyright-free illustrations called *Children in the Picture* (see Appendix 1: Booklist).

Check for copyright if you are using material from published sources; this is covered in Chapter 10.

Another possibility is to use computer graphics. There are now many computer programmes that offer a range of graphic designs. Some of these are on 'shareware' or 'public domain' programmes, which means you pay a low price or none at all for using them. To get good results with these you need a good printing process, as explained on pages 94–5. Without this, it's better not to try at all or only to use the very simplest of graphics.

Check how far it is possible to use *photographs* in your printing process, and the form in which they need to be. Many duplicators and photocopiers will not deal with them at all. Printers usually need photographs turned into 'half-tones', which means that the image is transformed into a series of tiny black dots. A printer may be able to do this him/herself, or tell you the name of a firm of plate-makers who can also blow up or shrink a photograph for you to fit the space.

Size and shape

The size and shape of what you are producing should be dictated by the use to which the publication is going to be put, and the image you are trying to get across. For instance:

- A membership card that you want people to carry around with them needs to be small enough to go into a wallet or a pocket.
- A leaflet that's to go into people's letter-boxes needs to be small enough to be folded twice, or at most four times. Design it so that

people can see who it is from and what it is about while it is still folded.

- A publication that's delivering 'hot news' to people (or trying to give that impression) might need to look like a newspaper. This then means producing it in 'tabloid' size – like the *Daily Mirror* or *Today*, rather than *The Guardian* – and using the same sort of paper.

- A report that you want to use as the 'showcase' for your organisation may need to be A4 size, so that you can include plenty of pictures and use the two halves of the book when it's open as a 'double page spread' with a striking design.

What paper to use

The right paper can make your message more or less effective, and also give a particular image to your organisation. A leaflet that is being given out in the street, for instance, needs heavier paper than one that is being put on chairs in a meeting room. A factcard that you want people to refer to often, and perhaps to keep in a dirty workplace, would need to be on hard-wearing glazed card. A fund-raising brochure needs to look attractive, but not so flashy that people wonder what you are using the money for. Recycled paper will be important to many groups. Printing in more than one colour can look good, but is expensive. But you may be able to achieve the same effect by using coloured card or paper as the background.

A printer, or a commercial stationer, should be able to show you samples of the various 'weights' and colours of the paper available. Explain exactly what you need it for, and check that it is suitable for the process you are going to use.

9

Production and printing

This is a summary of the main points to think about on the production side, when you are getting anything printed. For much fuller explanations and practical help, look at *Effective Publicity and Design*, by Jonathan Zeitlyn (for details see Appendix 1: Booklist). This is the best book on the subject for the lay person.

The various printing methods

The different methods of printing depend on the sort of equipment available. The main ones, starting from the least sophisticated, are:

- Duplicator.
- Photocopier.
- Bubble jet and laser printers.
- Offset litho printer.
- Photolith printer.

The last two are used mainly by professional printers; the first two are mainly for amateurs doing it themselves. The bubble jet and laser printers are available to both, and are breaking down the barriers between photocopying and printing, and between amateurs and professionals.

Most of these printing methods use photography at one stage or another, to transfer the image from the original to the new copies. So the original has to end up in the form of 'camera-ready copy' or CRC – that is, a piece of paper that is ready to be photographed and transferred. Getting to that stage involves *setting* the text, *laying out* and *pasting up*. Again, there are several ways to do this:

- Do it yourself, with scissors and glue.
- Do it yourself electronically, with a computer.
- Get it done by professional printers and typesetters.

The different methods have advantages and drawbacks. Which one is best will depend on:

- How many copies you want. Duplicating and photocopying are economical for a short 'run' of up to about 500 copies, but proper printing is cheaper for long runs.
- What the publication is. A single sided leaflet is simpler to produce than a 20 page report, so you could use 'do it yourself' methods more readily.
- What your skills are. Do it yourself methods need perfectionists to work well. If you haven't got any in your group, and can't find one for free, then you'll need to pay for one.
- How much time and energy, and how many willing helpers you have. If you've got enough neat careful volunteers, you can do the collating of a booklet or the folding of a leaflet yourselves and cut down the cost.
- What your budget is.

The cheapest method may not be the one that produces the results you want. Photocopying or duplicating on an unreliable machine, for instance, could lead to a lot of wastage (pushing up the real price) and a shabby end-product.

Discuss your problems with the professionals. A printer, for instance, may be able to suggest ways in which costs can be cut without sacrificing quality, for example, by using off-cuts and odd reams of paper.

Do it yourself methods

Duplicating

Duplicators are fairly cheap, and easily available. You can produce good material from them *if* you take the trouble, but it is also easy not to.

Electrostencil machines cut a stencil by a photographic process. Ask the local Council of Voluntary Services, or other groups, if they have one. Alternatively, a commercial printer or office services bureau could cut the stencil for you for a few pounds. You need to provide camera-ready copy as you would for a printer: see the section on layout, pages 92–3, for how to do this.

You can instead cut the stencil yourselves. For this you need a manual or electric typewriter with a good clear set of keys. Work out exactly what you want to go on to your piece of paper before you start preparing the stencil. Mistakes can be corrected, but each one increases the chances of the stencil turning out badly.

Headlines or drawings need to be cut by hand with a stylus, resting the stencil on a hard surface.

The duplicating process means that ink is forced through the holes in the stencil on to your piece of paper, so it works best if those holes are not too large. Bold black headlines and dark pictures tend to get smudged. So use outlines and line drawings instead. Very few duplicators will reproduce photographs, even if they have been turned into half-tones (explained on page 81).

It's possible to duplicate in more than one colour, but laborious. It's best to use two machines, each with different colour ink.

Duplicators are temperamental. Try to get someone to show you how a strange one works before you start. Give yourselves enough time and patience to do the work properly. The end product needs to be straight on the page, uncrumpled, and clean. There needs to be enough ink on the rollers to produce clear readable text.

With elderly machines, it could be wise to print on only one side of the paper, so that you do not have to send the sheets through the roller twice. A modern one, though, would find this no problem. Make sure you get the two sides the same way up!

If you make a mistake, or get poor results, throw the bad copies away. Anyone who is given one will probably be too annoyed to read it.

Photocopying

You can produce a very good result on a good photocopier, but it is not cheap, The real cost per copy, taking the rent and maintenance of the machine, and the running costs into account, is about 3p a copy. If you have to pay for it commercially, it may be a good deal more. So if you have to pay, it is economical only for small numbers of copies. However, many people can get free photocopies to some extent at least, and so for them it is cheaper than any other method. If you are borrowing a copier, *always* take your original away with you afterwards. Probably more secrets have been given away by people leaving the original under the cover of the copying machine than by any other method.

Alternatively, go to a copy shop. They can produce good results, and some have two-colour or even full-colour copiers. But they are not cheap. Specify exactly what you want done and get an estimate – including VAT where relevant – before you give the work to them. You may be able to save money, without losing quality, by such things as getting them to reduce the size of the print in a report so that two pages of typescript can fit on one side of paper, and by doing the collating yourselves.

Going to the professionals

Printers

You can find a printer by:

- Looking in the library, or local Council of Voluntary Service, for the addresses of community print-shops in your area. These are set up specifically to help community organisations, and will probably teach you how to use the equipment yourself.

- Talking to an organisation which has a lot of printing done, like the local Labour Party, about who they use. This has the advantage that the printers know that if they mess up your work, they will lose their reputation with two customers rather than one.

- Going through Yellow Pages and ringing up different printers, or going to see them. Tell them exactly what you want, and ask how much they will charge. If you don't know exactly what you want, ask for the most likely amount and size, so you can get a comparison.

Check what's available

The barriers between photocopying and printing are coming down. Computers mean that, increasingly, non-profit making organisations like resource centres can produce material that looks as if it has been commercially printed. There are certainly going to be more changes in the future. So keep a note of what is available, and at what price. Phone round to re-check with suppliers and printers whenever you have a major piece of work on. It could be helpful to keep a card index, or a file, listing the different services available, what they can do and who the contact person is.

If you have particular needs, like a source of half-tone blocks (explained on page 81) keep a note of these also. Knowing where to go quickly could make the difference between producing on time and missing your deadline.

Alternatively, the local Council of Voluntary Service, or a big user of print resources like the Labour Party might already be doing this, and let you pick their brains.

Once you have found someone good, offer them a ready supply of work for as long as they remain competitive and deliver the goods. If their standard seems to be slipping, complain. Ask for sub-standard work to be redone. If they don't improve, be hard hearted and move your custom elsewhere. Explain why – you could be doing them a service by pointing out where they are falling down.

To get the best results, you also need to be a good customer. Agree a schedule at the beginning, and stick to it. Turn up when you say you are going to, with work in the right form. If you are late, your publication will have to be given a new place in the queue of work. It will therefore fall behind schedule, probably by more days than have been lost.

Send the printers work which is clear, and with instructions that are easy to understand. This will speed up the process, and also save you money. Printers charge heavily for extra work that takes unexpected time.

There are two stages in getting your work ready. One is preparing the words and pictures that you want printed in draft form, and giving your instructions about what is to be done with it. The second stage is getting it to the final camera-ready copy stage, where the words and pictures are on pieces of paper looking exactly the way you want them printed. The first stage will always be up to you, and the second stage may well be too. Alternatively, you may hand over your draft to the professionals for them to get up to the final standard.

Preparing your draft
The preparation work is the same, whether you are carrying out the next stage yourselves or handing it over to others.

Always type your draft. Use a typewriter with a carbon ribbon, or a word processor with a daisy wheel printer, or a dot-matrix one set to 'near-letter quality'. If no one in your group owns such things, try to find someone who works in an office who can type out your work in the lunch hour. It needs to be in black, on one side only of clean A4 sheets of strong white paper. Number each sheet in the top right corner. Keep a copy of the original.

Leave two-inch margins all round; use double line spacing on the typewriter. Alter as little as you can on the typed copy. The more corrections there are, the more difficult it will be for the typesetters to follow. If you need to change words, cross out the original ones and write the replacements legibly above the crossing out. For other items, try to follow the list of proof-correction marks that printers use, shown on page 88–9. The full set of marks is published by British Standards Institution (BS 5261: Part 2: 1976). To take words out, score them through completely with a heavy black line. Put an X in the margin beside any line where there is a change.

Start each section on a new sheet. Show clearly where new paragraphs start, by indenting. That means moving the first word in by three spaces, as at the beginning of this paragraph. Do not break words by hyphens at the end of the line. Type them whole on the next line.

Proof-correction marks

Marginal mark	Meaning	Corresponding mark in text
⟍ᵒ⟋	Delete (take out)	/ Cross through
⟍ᵒ⟋	Delete and close-up	Above and below letters to be taken out
Ⓥ	Leave as printed (when matter has been crossed out by mistake)	….. Under characters to remain
≡	Change to capital letters	≡ Under letters or words altered
=	Change to small capitals	= Under letters or words altered
≠	Change capitals to lower case	⊂⟩ Encircle letters to be altered
⌴	Change to italics	— Under letters or words altered
⅄	Insert (or substitute) superior figure or sign	/ or ⋀
⅃	Insert (or substitute) inferior figure or sign	/ or ⋀
⊢⊣	Insert (or substitute) hyphen	/ or ⋀
⌒	Close-up — delete space	⌒ Linking words or letters
⅄	Insert space	| or ⅄ Between characters/ words

Marginal mark	Meaning	Corresponding mark in text
—(or)—	Insert space between lines or paragraphs	
→ or ⟨	Reduce space between lines or paragraphs	
⌐⌐	Transpose	⌐⌐ Between letters or words, numbered when necessary
5	Transpose lines	5
[ ]	Place in centre of line	[ ] Around matter to be centred
(a) ⟨E	Move to (a) the left	(a) ⅂
(b) ⊐→⏐	(b) the right	(b) ⌐
⌐	Begin a new paragraph	Before first word of new paragraph
⊃	No fresh paragraph here	⊂⊃ Between paragraphs
⋏	(Caret mark.) Insert matter indicated in margin	⋏
⅋⅋⅋	Insert single/double quotes	⋏ ⋏
‖	Correct vertical alignment	‖
⊐	Indent	⊐
⊏	Cancel indent	⊢

Specification

This means giving instructions about how the copy is to be set out. The clearer and fuller the instructions are, the easier the job is and the quicker it will be done. Write the instructions clearly on the typed copy, in a different colour, preferably red.

Underline words in the typescript if you want them set in *italic*; put a wavy line underneath if you want them **bold**.

Points to think about, for yourselves or a typesetter, are:

- how long the lines are;
- what size the margins are;
- how far the apart the lines are (called linespacing);
- the typeface; and
- the type size.

Talk to the professionals about how you want your work to look, and what they can do. Most will be glad to advise you, as it will make their job easier. There is usually a catalogue giving examples of different typefaces, sizes, linespacings and layouts. They may show you examples of other work too. You *can* change your mind once you see a completed proof copy, but it will cost you money.

If you are doing it yourself, explore what is available on your typewriter, word processor or computer package, or look at catalogues of Letraset or other dry transfer lettering (explained below). Fix your ideas at this stage and try not to change them. Doing so is bound to cost you time, and may well also cost money, if you have to buy new software or new sheets of lettering.

Different typefaces and layouts will give a different image to your group. Look critically at the possibilities, and decide which fits your objectives better.

Decide whether you want gaps between the paragraphs, and if so, how wide. If you are quoting someone else's words, do you want them in a smaller type size, or in italic, or indented?

Do you want your right margin justified, that is, in a straight line (as in this book) or ragged? What size are your headings and sub-headings to be? If you want several different sizes, mark the headings A, B, and C to show the different sizes. How much space do you want before and after the headings? Do you want them on the left or right of the page, or 'centred' (that is, in the middle).

What colour is the print to be? If you are using more than one colour, which words are in which colour?

There is a full explanation of all these points in *Effective Publicity and Design* (see Appendix 1: Booklist)

Style

Before giving the copy to the typesetter, you need to decide on and mark up the punctuation; to decide on when capital letters are to be used in headings; the treatment of abbreviation signs and figures (for example, are you using % or 'per cent', & or 'and', 6 or 'six'); whether you want to put quotations in single or double quotation marks; whether you want initials written as, for instance, CPAG or C.P.A.G.

It is best to avoid using '&' if you can, and to write out numbers up to ten in full, using figures for larger numbers. 'Per cent' is rather clumsy, so use % instead.

Decide on these points before you start, and then check on the finished copy that you have been consistent.

Proofreading

This means checking the text carefully for any mistakes. It should be done several times. The first check should come before you send the material to the typesetters. Once they have set up your text, any alterations you ask for will cost extra as 'author's corrections'. Get people who have not been involved in the drafting to go through the draft with a fresh eye. It is easy, for instance, to leave out a 'not' in some crucial place. The person who has done the writing may be unable to spot it because they are too familiar with the work.

Depending on the processes you are using, you may be sent 'galleys' and then 'page-proofs' or simply 'page-proofs'. Galleys are the text set up in the way it will look on the page, but not split into the pages or numbered. Sometimes they come as long strips of paper with many pages on each, but more often now they are ordinary pages. You may find that the same few lines are printed at the bottom of one page and the top of the next; don't worry about this, as it won't happen with the real text.

Go through carefully and look for spelling mistakes, places where the words have been jumbled, and other errors; check carefully that the figures in tables are right, and that the various columns are in the right places. Mark the mistakes on the text, with the special marks shown on pages 88–9. These should be corrected by the typesetter before the next stage.

'Page-proofs' are made either by the typesetter on screen, or by you, by cutting up the galleys and laying them out on the page in the design you have chosen, with any headings and pictures included. Even if you have already read through the galleys carefully to check for mistakes, do so again at this stage. Make sure that the points you marked last time have been taken into account, and that no new mistakes, like putting paragraphs in the wrong order, have crept in. With a long document, you also need to put in the right page numbers for any cross references here, and also in your table of contents and index, if you have them.

When you are satisfied, the text goes to the printing firm and is run off, or you can print it yourself. If you are using separate typesetting and printing firms, the typesetter will give you the finished product – the camera ready copy or artwork – to take to the printer. Keep this in an envelope or plastic folder. Dirty marks on it will show up in the printing.

Paste up and layout

If you are doing the typesetting yourself, using a computer package, you will probably be able to do the layout on the screen as well, as explained on page 97. Other people may need to do the paste up and layout by hand. This is not difficult, but it requires patience, neat fingers, and the right equipment. You will need:

- Layout sheets. These are sheets of plain paper with squares ruled on them in a very faint blue, to help you keep your columns straight. The blue does not show up in the final printing.

- Clear plastic ruler and set square.

- A soft rubber to clean the artwork. The best thing for this is a ball of congealed Cow Gum (see below).

- A black pen – a good clear felt- or fibre-tip will do – and a light blue pencil for ruling your own lines.

- A way of typing out your text in clear black letters. You can do this on a manual or electric typewriter, with a new ribbon in it and very clean keys. An electronic typewriter, or a high quality printer (see below for more details of these) working from a computer, will produce a very good image.

- Dry transfer lettering, such as Letraset or Meccanorm (from a stationer's or art suppliers) for your headlines. Work out carefully what you need, and stick to one or two styles, as you have to buy complete sheets at a time. Or you can use a machine which prints the letters out on a strip of transparent paper (a Kroy or P-touch machine). See if any local group has one. They are coming down in price and are well worth investing in. Several groups could club together to buy one, if necessary.

- White correcting fluid, so you can paint over mistakes and marks. The water-based versions are better for your health.

- Sharp scissors and a Stanley knife, scalpel or razor to cut things out and paste them on your layout sheet.

- Glue. The best sort is called Cow Gum (because the inventor was a Henry Cow). It lets you slide the bits of artwork around before finally sticking them down.

- A layout board, or another smooth hard surface, such as a piece of glass or a formica table-top, to work on. A Stanley knife will cut into wood, so don't use furniture.

If you do not have some of these, and do not want to buy them, try borrowing them from:

a community printshop;

a resource centre;

the local community newspaper;

another local group who produce their own newsletter; or

the art or design department of the local secondary school or college.

Work out your own design, and do a rough version first. Then make sure that you have got everything you need together.

Decide on the width of your columns, and type out your text carefully to fit. Assemble copies of the cartoons, pictures, and graphics you intend to use. Work out what headlines you want, and put them on to a separate piece of paper. Rule a light blue line to act as your guide. If there are cracks in the lettering, touch them up with a black pen. Check everything carefully for mistakes.

Now cut out the different items. Lay them out on the layout sheet, without any glue, check they all fit, and finally stick them on the layout sheet.

Cover any lines that show with correcting fluid, and rub out pencil marks and other dirty marks. Then keep your artwork carefully in a folder until it is time to print it.

Using a computer

Many people now have their own computers, or access to them at work. They can be a great help in the layout and printing processes, but they can also waste time and energy, and end up providing shabby results. This is only a brief summary of the possibilities and problems. See Charles Foster's book (see Appendix 1: Booklist) for more information.

Preparing a draft

For preparing a draft copy, even the simplest computer with a word processing program and printer is useful.

If no one in your group has computer skills, look for someone who uses computers in their office, or for a son or daughter who has learned about them in school. Prepare your text, and ask them to put it onto the screen for you. Get them to explain the process as they go along, so that you can do it yourself next time.

You may find you can write your draft straight on to the computer screen. The program will allow you to delete words, move them around, add extra words half way through the text, and so on. If you are unfamiliar with the machine, it's probably better to work out the wording on a piece of paper to start with. Then copy-type it onto the screen.

Always save and print out each piece of work as you do it – *and* make a back-up copy on another disk, even if you know there's further work to be done later. If you have a copy, it will be less of a tragedy when some idiot puts their coffee cup down on the disk.

Many word processing packages have spelling checkers built into them. Use these by all means, but proofread as well. The spelling checker won't pick up missing words. It will also not notice words that are spelt correctly, but which have been used in the wrong context, for instance, putting 'witch', when you mean 'which'. Computers are programmed to follow their own set of rules, not to read your mind. Many spell checkers use American spelling, though with the better ones it is possible to add the English version into the dictionary yourself.

If your work is going to a typesetter, you will still need to *mark up* by hand, as explained on pages 90–91.

Most typesetting and printing firms are computerised themselves now, and will find it helpful to work from a copy of your computer disk if you have one. Check with them what form they need it in, and whether they can deal with the program you have been using. Send them the printed-out copy *and* the disk, and keep spare copies of both yourself. This is important, because the ones you send may get lost, and also because you may need to refer to them in answering queries.

There are special computer programs for marking up, but it is not worth trying to obtain one unless you intend to do a great deal of publishing.

Setting the text on the computer

Almost any computer program can be used to create lines of the right length, and 'justified' (explained on page 90). But you need the right *printer*, to produce text which is good enough to paste up.

There are four main sorts of computer printer: dot-matrix, daisy wheel, bubble jet and laser. Dot matrix printers create each letter as a series of tiny dots. Most of them – including those sold with the Amstrad PCW systems – are 'nine-pin'. They are good enough for printing out drafts, but little more. The print tends to be rather faint, unless you make it near-letter quality, which means that the machine goes over each letter twice. Once printed, the separation of the dots shows up, and gives a rather poor result. Computer graphics, or any sort of fancy printing, will look rough and ready.

Twenty-four-pin printers give a much better result. Text and graphics can look good printed on the best of these. You may be able to vary your typeface with them, and to print in different scripts, such as Greek and Cyrillic.

Daisy wheel printers and electronic typewriters hooked up to computers will usually give very good print results. But they won't be able to do graphics, and changing the typeface will mean changing the daisy wheel. It is not impossible, just rather laborious.

Laser printers work on the same technology as photocopiers, and so produce a result which looks as good or better. They can easily go wrong, though, and are also expensive, so few community organisations have them. They are much faster and quieter than the other sorts of printer, and the best can produce anything that a professional printer can do. The most expensive laser printers include 'Postscript'. This is the trade name for a built-in program that makes it almost into a computer on its own, and smoothes out the rough edges of curves. It will produce text and pictures that can look as if they have come from a book.

It would be worth several groups getting together and sharing a laser printer, perhaps via the Council of Voluntary Service or the Trades Council, if they can raise the money to do so. Otherwise, you should be able to find a computer service bureau or a copy shop that will print your work on its own equipment, or a local desktop publishing firm that will take your disk and print it out for you. Look in Yellow Pages for details. It is also worth trying local schools and colleges. If they have the right equipment, they will often let others use it for a small charge.

To create different typefaces on a laser printer you need different 'fonts'. These come on separate 'cards' (actually small squares of plastic with microchips embedded in them). Sometimes there is only one font to a card, sometimes several. If there is only one to a card, you will not be able to use more than one typeface to a page. But you can still vary the size, and make the print bold or italic.

Bubble jet printers can create the same quality of print as a laser printer, and are much cheaper. But they are rather slower, and only just becoming widely available. You'll need to check that the computer program you are using will work with a bubble jet.

Points to check with any printer

Check before you start:

- whether your own computer program will allow you to create 'proportional spacing'; and

- how well or badly it 'justifies' when you are typing in columns.

'Proportional spacing' means that different letters are given different amounts of space on a page; a letter 'i' for instance, will take up less room than an 'm'. Without this, when you justify the right margin in narrow columns, there will only be a few words to a line, with big spaces between them.

So if the machine doesn't do proportional spacing, it would be better to have a ragged margin, so that the words themselves look neater and are easier to read.

Most computers are sold as being 'wysiwyg'. This mysterious word stands for 'what you see [on the screen] is what you get'. In other words, what comes out on the paper looks the same as what is on the screen. Very few of them actually are. Check this on your equipment, and see what the differences are, before you start doing the layout.

Work within your limits

Find out the capacity of the computer and printer you have access to, and work within it. If, for instance, you can produce good text, but poor pictures, then don't try pictures on it. Draw freehand, trace or photocopy from the special books instead. Don't be tempted to use the gimmicks that are available just because they are there.

Compatibility

Before you spend any time typing in your precious work, check that the printer and the computer are 'compatible' – that is, that they will cooperate with each other. Only too often the equipment itself will work perfectly, but the 'interface' – the program that joins the different parts together – plays up, or won't communicate what you want to communicate. So run off some test pieces first, and see how they come out at the other end. Type in any old rubbish, but include the characters machines often have trouble with, like the '£' or '!'.

If something won't work, check all the obvious points first. Is everything switched on, has the connector plug worked loose, have you given it the right commands? Then if it still doesn't work, *either* find a real expert who plays happily with it for hours while you are in the pub, *or* give up altogether and go to the pub anyway. Don't try to fiddle around with it unless you really know what you are doing. You can waste hours, ruin your eyesight and your temper, possibly mess up someone else's program, and still get nowhere. Go back to old-fashioned typewriters instead.

Full desktop publishing

This means that you do all the layout and paste up on your computer, rather than on a piece of paper.

The programs take up a great deal of space on a computer disk, but any machine that is IBM compatible, and has a double disk drive or a hard disk ought to be OK. You can produce acceptable results on a fairly ordinary computer and a 24-pin dot matrix printer; but for the best results you need a Postscript laser printer, as explained above.

It often takes some time to get used to a desktop publishing (DTP) program, so don't start experimenting with it when you have a tight deadline to meet. Working with a 'mouse' (a way of moving the pointer on the computer by rolling a small ball on the table) takes time to learn as well, and you need good hand-to-eye coordination.

Computer programs can't turn you into brilliant designers or layout artists. They make it easier for you to do what you want to. But if the design you want to produce is a mess, then what comes out of the computer will be a mess too. Work out your layout roughly, with a pen and paper, and then transfer it on to the computer. When you are satisfied with what's on the screen, print it out, and proofread just as you would with any other piece of paper. It is even easier to miss out words, or to misspell words and not notice, on a computer screen than it is on paper. Only when you are finally satisfied should you run off the copies.

You may well find that although the copies look good, the printer is extremely slow at producing them. It is usually better to produce just one master set, and then find someone with a high definition photo-copier – something rather better than in the average copy shop – to do as many copies as you need.

Finding out more

There are plenty of computer-literate people around. Unfortunately many of them are bad at translating what they know into words the rest of us can understand. The people who write computer manuals are particu-larly bad at this. If you want to find out more, or to try to work out ways in which your group can use a computer, there are several sources to try:

- Local computing resource centres. There are only a few of these. One example is Community Computing in Newcastle, which has a number of different computers and laser printers. They run courses, lay out and produce newsletters and other printed material for community groups, and will show people how to use the computers so that they can do the work themselves. Other groups like them are linked by the Community Computing Network (see Appendix 2: Addresses): contact them to see if there is one in your area.

- The local technical college, polytechnic, or university may have people in the computing department, or the Art and Design department, who can help. Make sure the person advising you does know about your area. Many computer specialists are interested mainly in mathematics, and will know no more about desktop publishing than you do. They may also need to charge you for their time, to balance their department's books.

- The people who teach computing at the local secondary school *may* know a lot about computers – or they may be just one step ahead of the students. But they are quite likely to have found someone themselves to solve their problems.

- There may be someone in your office who does the sort of work that you are trying to produce on your machine. Look around at the sort of printed documents that are being produced, and ask who did the work on them.

- See if there's a user group for your particular equipment. Most of the major types of computer have their own clubs. Look in the computer magazines for their addresses, and then talk to the Secretary to find out if they can help you. Many clubs run helplines which allow people who are having problems to get in touch with other more experienced users. They cost £20 to £30 a year.

- Ask someone under the age of 15. There are juvenile computer whizz-kids all over the place. You may have to bribe them with a computer game, and you will also have to assess whether they really know what they are talking about, or just boasting. But there's no need to feel humiliated about asking their advice. After all, if you had been playing with computers since you were five, you would be just as good.

Courses

If you are planning to do a lot of work on a computer, it will be worth going on a course. Ask around for details of one that others recommend. Many universities and colleges run residential summer schools, lasting perhaps a week at a time at a reasonable cost. Alternatively, there are both commercial and non-profit making groups who do training.

Check carefully that any course really *is* what you want. Some courses are advertised as being for beginners, but if they have been running for some time they may have attracted a group of experienced regulars who could get impatient with you. Study the literature, and if necessary phone the tutor or organiser and ask questions.

If you can't find a course that suits you, contact a tutor who has been recommended to you, and ask if they could design a course that is what you want. If the cost is beyond you, join up with several other groups to share it, or put something in your grant application next year to cover the cost.

Be demanding. If a course is above your head, say so, and ask for the points to be explained again more clearly. If you are not getting enough time to practise what you want, say so again. If you don't understand, that's not your fault – it's the tutor's. His or her skill is supposed to be putting knowledge across to you – if it's not happening, then where's the skill?

Checklists

---

1. Getting things printed; decisions before you start

What's it for?
How is it being distributed?
When must it be ready by?
How many copies?
How much are you spending?
Design (rough sketch)

Size and shape ....
Paper weight..
Colour ....
Print colour(s) ....

---

2. Who's doing what?

Task	Who'll do it	By when
writing the words		
typing out the draft		
proof reading at this stage		
design		
giving typesetting instructions		
setting the text		
creating graphics or pictures		
proof reading at this stage		
laying out and pasting up		
proof reading again		
printing final copy		
folding		
collating		
stapling or binding		

Special points to bear in mind...
....
....
....
....
....
....
....
....
....
....
....

3. Getting it typeset and printed; quotations sought

Name of firm ....

Name of contact person...

Address..

Phone number...

For [details of work to be done] ....

....

Delivery by [date]...

Quotation given [including VAT]...

Weight of paper...

Colour ....

Coated or not ....

Galleys due on [date] ....

To be returned by [date]..

Final proofs due on [date] ....

To be returned by [date]..

To be collected or sent?...

Any other comments ....

....

....

....

....

....

....

....

....

....

....

....

4. Specification for the typesetter

Trimmed size of page.............................mm. Pages (approx) ....

Typeface to be used...

Size leading of type and spacing of main headings ....

subheadings..

ordinary text ....

Paragraph indent ....

Width of main type area...

10

The law

This Chapter covers the law about printing and publishing in general. Special areas are dealt with in the relevant Chapters. Thus the law on distributing leaflets publicly comes in Chapter 11; that on flyposting is covered in Chapter 11; that on various special rules about radio and television is covered in Chapters 20 and 21. The voluntary codes of practice journalists are *supposed* to be bound by, and the way they can be enforced, are covered in Chapter 21.

Neither this Chapter, nor the other sections, are detailed enough to rely on. If you seem to be getting into legal trouble, you *must* consult a solicitor, however difficult it will be to pay the bill. If you get taken to court, or even threatened with it, it could cost you a great deal more. Ask for legal advice under the Green Form Scheme to start with. If the problem stems from something related to your work (and in some other cases as well) you should be able to get free advice from your union.

Copyright

This means the property right that a person has in what they have written or designed. In law, you are entitled to quote a few words or sentences without permission, but you should say what the source is. If your quote is longer than a few sentences, you need to ask permission, and you may need to pay a fee. This also applies to pictures, cartoons and graphics, including those on computer. Any item can be made 'out of copyright' by the originator. There are books of illustrations and disks of computer graphics which are published specifically so that people can use them. For instance, Journeyman Press publish a book of graphics *Children in the Picture*, which is copyright free.

There are also some documents, especially official ones, which include a statement like this:

The text of this announcement may be freely reproduced in newspapers, magazines, etc, provided the source is acknowledged.

You would then be free to quote it in full, saying where it came from. But otherwise, look for the word 'Copyright' and a name, or a C in a circle like this © which is the code. This will tell you who owns the copyright.

Fifty years after an author's death, the words come out of copyright. So you can reproduce Dickens or Shakespeare freely, but not a modern author. If in doubt, check. Some people live a very long time. All Irving Berlin's 1930s songs, for example, will still be in copyright because he only died recently, aged over 100. J M Barrie left the copyright of all his works, including Peter Pan, to Great Ormond Street Hospital for ever. Certain authors' literary estates are very carefully controlled. If you are in any doubt, check with the last publisher.

If you think you need permission, write to the copyright holders. If you don't know the address, write to the publisher and ask them to forward your letter. Chase it up if you don't receive an answer. Newspapers and magazines are usually happy for you to reproduce their tables and graphs, provided you acknowledge the source. Cartoonists may let you reprint their picture, especially if they agree with your cause, but they might want to be paid.

Freelance photographers and picture agencies make their living by letting out reproduction rights, so they will certainly want a fee and will pursue you if you do not arrange this before you use their work.

Commercial organisations are also careful about use of their trade marks, or of anything that is recognisably theirs. For instance, if you use a picture of a Disney character like Mickey Mouse or Donald Duck, sooner or later the Disney empire will catch up with you, and ask for their reproduction fee, which is high.

Companies can also take action against you for wrongful use of a registered trade name. These must be printed with capital letters, and you may need permission to use them. Examples are Coca Cola and Sellotape. A list of trade names can be found in the *UK Press Gazette*, but it is not complete. If in doubt, check with the company.

Include details of the copyright holder on anything important that you publish, and insist that other people acknowledge their source if they quote you. This will help to build up your group's reputation. If the people who want to quote you are well-off – like a television programme or a national newspaper – you might also want to ask for a fee. But if you are keen to be quoted, it might be better not to insist as it may put some people off.

Credit any original drawings or photographs separately in your publications, or in displays. Then either you, or the people who created them, can ask for a reproduction fee if others want to use them.

Passing off

You can be sued if you 'pass off' someone else's work as your own, or if you are the publisher of something that another person is passing off as their own. You must be aware, though, that you are infringing the law, before you are liable.

You could be threatened with legal action for passing off if you produce something that was intended to look like another publication – a spoof copy of the *News of the World,* for instance. Your defence would be that it could not possibly have deceived anyone, so make it an obvious spoof. For example, you could make its headline 'Not the News of the World.'

Imprints

Anything printed must by law have an 'imprint' – that is, the name and address of the printer and publisher – on each copy. The penalties for forgetting this are not very great. The printer has to keep a copy of each piece of work done, together with a record of who asked for the work, and can be prosecuted for not doing so.

Defamation

This is the most serious problem, because of the potential cost of an action against you. It's possible to run up large bills without going to court, by having to consult solicitors and barristers about the threat of a writ which may not even turn up.

'Defamation' covers both slander and libel. Slander is defamation in speech; libel is defamation in writing, drawings, cartoons, photographs and broadcasting. Most cases are about 'civil' slander or libel. This means that one individual brings a case against others. Authors, printers and publishers can all be sued. You may be able to get free or cheap legal advice when threatened with a case, but you cannot get legal aid if it goes to court.

You libel a person by publishing something untruthful that tends to lower him/her in the estimation of society; to make him/her hated, ridiculed or disliked by society; or to make people feel contemptuous of him/her or to avoid his/her company. 'Society' means conventional, 'right-thinking' people. You don't need to imply that a person is at fault for it to be libellous. Saying someone had been mentally ill might be seen as libellous, even though it is not their fault.

'Publishing' means communicating to anyone else. So you can libel someone by circulating the proofs of a leaflet before it is ever published. But if someone stopped it at that stage because they had realised the dangers, this could be taken into account when the damages are worked out.

A printer may refuse to print what you have written if s/he believes it to be libellous.

A letter can also be libellous: on Tyneside in 1990, a firm called Press Offshore issued writs against six shop stewards over the contents of a letter they had written to the firm's clients, though it did not pursue the matter further.

The person claiming to have been libelled is called the 'plaintiff'. Plaintiffs do not have to show that any actual harm has been done, but they do have to show that the material refers to them, or could be taken as doing so. So you might unintentionally libel someone by referring to someone *else* by a nickname that they also used. A general comment could be libellous if you mentioned someone's name in conjunction with it. For instance, if you said, 'Only criminals go to X club; Mr P was seen there last Wednesday,' you would be libelling Mr P. You can also libel by 'innuendo', which means that what you are implying but not actually saying is defaming that person. An example of this is, 'a person not a million miles from Mr P was seen handing money over to a policeman.'

If you libel one unnamed person in a small identifiable group, each person in that group could take you to court. So if you said that one of the board of directors was stupid or dishonest, without saying who you mean, any or all of them could take you to court.

Defending yourself

You can defend yourself:

- By showing that what you said is fully justified, that is, that it was true (not just that you believed it was).

- By showing that the words were 'fair comment' – that it was an opinion, not malicious, about a matter of public concern. This cannot be used about a person's moral character. It needs to be a genuinely held opinion, based on facts stated elsewhere in the same publication.

- By absolute privilege. MPs and judges can say more or less what they like in Parliament and the courts.

- By qualified privilege. This covers people reporting court cases fairly and accurately, Parliament and public meetings. With the report of a public meeting, if the person concerned asks the reporter or the newspaper to publish a letter of explanation, and they refuse, this defence cannot be used. Only straight reporting of Parliament is covered; the fact that an MP has made an accusation against someone in Parliament does not mean that you can repeat it safely. You also have qualified privilege for statements made in discharge of a public or private duty – for instance, when writing a reference.

- By claiming innocent defamation. This means saying that you did not mean to be defamatory and took reasonable care to avoid making the mistake. It is important to make an offer of amends as soon as possible. This would mean publishing a correction and an apology, and possibly offering a donation to 'a favourite charity.' An example of this would be if you referred to one person by name or by their nickname, and another person with the same name or nickname took it as being aimed at them.

If none of these defences are likely to succeed then, before a case gets to court, you can state that the libel was published without malice or gross negligence, and offer to publish a full apology. You may also need to offer money. If the plaintiff accepts, the case would not then need to go to court. But the amount you pay could be considerable.

Under the law of civil (though not criminal) libel a dead person cannot be defamed. But you still have to be careful in case some of those involved in a particular case are still alive.

Checking for libel

If you are exposing a scandal, even in very mild terms, or making allegations about individuals or groups, get a solicitor to check your text for libel. *Pay* for this, even if s/he is a friend who donates the fee back to you. Under their professional code of practice, if solicitors don't take a fee they usually do not have a liability for the advice they give you. So you can't take action against them, or claim against your own insurance or theirs, if their advice turns out to be wrong.

Libel is a specialised part of the law. Find the local expert by asking the local newspaper who checks their stories, or the branch secretary of the NUJ.

You can insure against libel, though it is not cheap. If you are publishing reports, newsletters or magazines which might include controversial material, you'd be wise to take out insurance.

Damages

When cases come to court, the jury decides not only whether there has been a libel, but also how much damages are payable. These twelve people may have very little idea of what is a reasonable amount, and may have memories of the big libel damages in well-publicised cases like that taken by Jeffrey Archer, so there is a risk that damages will be huge.

Sometimes juries give damages as one single sum. This is intended to compensate for the loss of reputation. They can add an extra amount for 'aggravated damages' if they think the defendant has behaved spitefully. They can also give 'exemplary' or 'punitive' damages, intended to punish someone who publishes a libel hoping that they will make money from extra sales.

Alternatively, the jury may decide that the plaintiff involved 'brought it on themselves' by their behaviour or their previous reputation. They can then judge that they are entitled only to 'nominal' damages. Or the judge can say that each side must carry its own costs. That would mean that even if you have won, you have very heavy bills to meet.

Slander

This applies to the spoken rather than the written word. Cases are much less common than libel cases. For anyone to prove that they have been slandered, they have to show that their reputation (defined in the same way as for libel) has been damaged. There are four things, though, that are slanderous simply by being said, even if there is no effect on the person's reputation:

- That someone has committed a criminal offence serious enough to be punishable by death or imprisonment.

- Allegations of 'unchastity or adultery' – but only if they are made against a woman.

- Imputing that at the time of the slander, someone has an contagious or infectious disease.

- Alleging something calculated to disparage a person in their office, trade or profession at the time of saying it.

When you are appearing on radio or television in a recorded programme, the interviewers themselves will probably remove any slanderous statements, but if the programme is going out live, there is little that you or they can do. So don't accuse individuals of things you can't prove. If you repeat a defamatory statement that someone else has made, you make yourself equally liable. Or you may be creating a slander that did not exist to start with, because the previous person hedged their bets and you have not.

Criminal prosecutions

It is possible – though very rare – to be taken to court for criminal libel. There are some differences in the law between this and the ordinary civil libel. You are fined rather than paying damages, you can be imprisoned for up to two years, you can defame someone even if you only make the comment to him or her, and you can defame someone even if they are dead. It's even more important to get good legal advice, if you are threatened with a prosecution for this. Legal aid for someone to defend you in court *is* available here.

You can also be prosecuted for:

- Publishing a false statement about the character of a candidate in a Parliamentary or local election, or about something that they have done, even if the statement is not libellous.

- Publishing something that's considered obscene under the Obscene Publications Act 1959. This is defined as material that would tend to deprave and corrupt people who are likely to read, see and hear it. There are not many prosecutions for this, but it has been used against gay groups in the past. The law can also be used to harass people, if the police or the Customs and Excise decide to seize material because they consider it obscene.

- Publishing something 'seditious' – which means something intended to incite contempt or hatred for the Queen or for Parliament, or to encourage people to overthrow the government by violent means. Prosecutions for this are very rare, partly because any government knows that the people concerned would be able to use the courts as a platform for their views, and could not be sure that a jury would convict.

- Publishing something that incites to racial hatred. This is an offence under the Race Relations Act 1976. The author's intention does not matter – you have committed an offence by publishing threatening, abusive or insulting matter that is likely to stir up hatred against any racial group in Great Britain. Again there have been very few prosecutions, even in what look like straightforward cases of speeches by people on the far right.

- Finally, you can be prosecuted for *blasphemous libel*. This means publishing something 'so scurrilous and offensive as to pass the limit of decent controversy and outrage any Christian feelings.' Of all the religions in this country, it's only Christianity which is protected in this way. There have been calls for the law to be extended to other religions, and other calls for it to be abolished altogether.

If you are threatened under any of the headings in this section, get in touch with *Liberty* (formerly the National Council for Civil Liberties) as well as taking legal advice.

Leaking documents

In the course of your campaigning activities, or your ordinary work, you could come across information that you are not supposed to have. If it strengthens the case you are putting forward, or shows up the people you are opposing, you may want to publish it.

You and the journalist who takes your story both run legal risks in doing this. The journalist may decide to reveal who told him or her the story, rather than go to prison. You may then find yourself in serious trouble.

Non-governmental information

The chief weapons for private companies or individuals are the *law of confidence* and the *Contempt of Court Act 1981*. The law of confidence is part of the common law (not laid down by an Act of Parliament) about the duties that employees owe towards their employers. In some cases, the employer can sue people for damages if they let out confidential information, even after they have left that employment, if their contract lays this down.

This law was used by British Steel, for example, when in 1980 Granada used leaked documents in a television programme. British Steel asked for a court order against Granada, ordering them to reveal who had done the leaking. Granada would not identify the source, but the judges – in a case which went right up to the House of Lords – said that they must.

Parliament then passed the Contempt of Court Act 1981. Section 10 of this says that:

> No court may require a person to disclose, nor is any person guilty of contempt of court for refusing to disclose, the source of information contained in a publication for which he [sic] is responsible, unless it is established to the satisfaction of the court that disclosure is necessary in the interests of justice or national security, or for the prevention of disorder or crime.

However, the judges have now decided that this protection means almost nothing. In November 1989 a journalist was leaked some information about the business affairs of a small engineering company. The article he wrote was never actually published, because the company took out an injunction against him, on the basis that it might harm their business. The judge said that the journalist must reveal who had told him, and he refused. The House of Lords said that it was up to judges to decide, in any particular case, whether section 10 was to protect the journalists or not. The fact that the journalist in this case was trying to write a news story about the company was a 'wholly unjustified intrusion.' He was fined £5,000. Luckily, his newspaper stood by him, and could afford to pay the fine and his legal costs.

If a document 'falls into your hands' when you do not have a direct relationship with the organisation concerned – for instance, if you see something interesting when you are in someone else's office by chance, and pocket it – you do not owe them any duty of confidence, but you could be prosecuted for theft instead.

Government information

The government can use the same laws as the private sector. People doing research for government departments, such as the DSS, are all covered by the law of confidence. So if they pass over their research findings to a pressure group without permission, for instance, they could be sued for breach of confidence.

In addition, the government will often be able to quote 'national security'. In 1983, for instance, *The Guardian* was ordered to return a document that had been leaked from the Ministry of Defence. This meant that they could identify the person who had leaked it, Sarah Tisdall, and she went to prison as a result.

The new Official Secrets Act 1989 says that revealing certain types of information without being authorised to do so is a criminal offence.

For some categories, the prosecution has to show that harm was done, or was likely to be the result, because the information was revealed. For others, revealing the information is an *absolute offence* even if it made no difference to anyone. Both the government employees who do the leaking and the journalists (or ordinary members of the public) who report the information, can be prosecuted.

There are different rules for various categories of information:

- Information about the security and intelligence services. For anyone who has worked in these services, or is a contractor who has been notified that they are covered, to give out unauthorised information is an absolute offence. For other people, disclosing the facts is an offence if harm has been done, or would be likely to be the result.

- Information about acts done under the new Security Services Act such as telephone tapping, interception of mail, or breaking into premises. Telling the facts on these matters is an absolute offence. The only way you could defend yourself would be to say that you did not realise, and had no reasonable cause to believe, that these were facts that came under these rules.

- Information about defence matters. The prosecution has to show that giving out this information had prejudiced, or would be likely to prejudice, the armed forces.

- Information about international relations. Here, the prosecution has to show that it would be likely to jeopardise the interests of the UK abroad. This could cover almost anything, from a proposal to close an embassy to a suggestion of reallocating overseas aid.

- Confidential information that has been obtained from another state or international organisation. *Liberty* in their briefing say that it might be an offence to publish a leak from the European Commission about pollution control or VAT.

- Information which leads (or could lead) to someone else committing a crime, allows someone to escape or impedes the prevention of a crime.

It is no defence to say that the information has already been published elsewhere, if the offence is one of the 'absolute' ones. Where there's a test of whether harm has been committed or not, the person doing the publishing has to weigh up whether a jury would think that enough harm has already been committed, so that repeating the information wouldn't do any more.

Finally, the Act does not allow you to use the defence that it was in the public interest to disclose the information. So you cannot say that publishing it prevented worse harm from being done, because it prevented a crime or an abuse of authority.

Anyone who is prosecuted, or threatened with prosecution, should contact *Liberty* for advice.

Who is liable under the law?

More than one person may be liable in law; including:

- the person who provides the information;
- the person who writes the story; and
- the group that is responsible for the publication.

They could all be committing an offence, or have a civil case brought against them. The printers and distributors may sometimes also have threats made against them, for instance in a libel case. These are very rarely followed up, but make printers very reluctant to accept work on which a writ could be issued.

If it ever got as far as a court case, it would almost certainly be an individual – probably the author – who faced the court. The group would then need to decide whether to stand behind him or her, and pay the court costs and any fine. The alternative would be to disclaim responsibility, which is a serious thing to do to a friend or colleague!

The risks you run

Anyone who wants to leak anything needs to think about what the consequences would be if they were found out, and whether they are prepared to risk them. You could well lose your job, and in some cases go to prison. Can you cope with that?

You might be able to conceal your identity when you leak, while still making clear that the information comes from a source to be trusted. You could obliterate your name as the person who received the memo, for instance, or the number which identifies which copy it is.

Technology has made this more difficult, however. In some cases where documents are intended to be confidential, a slightly different version is produced on the word processor for each person, so it is possible to identify where each copy came from.

An alternative is to show a journalist the document, let him or her read it, but then insist on taking it away afterwards. He or she may not be too happy about this, though, and may refuse to publish unless you pass over the papers.

PART III
Types of publication

11

Leaflets and posters

Leaflets

Leaflets are useful in various ways. They can:

- Reinforce a message that's being given face to face.
- Contain the main points someone's been making in a speech, to digest afterwards.
- Be handed out in the street, to alert people to something that is going to happen, or to a campaign which they might not hear about otherwise.
- Be pushed through people's letter-boxes, or left on their desks in an office, to give information about what is happening.
- Be posted or hand delivered, personally addressed, to a selected number of people.

If you are handed a leaflet in the street, or on your way into work, you're likely to glance at it and then thrust it into a bag or a pocket. If it catches your eye sufficiently, you may take it out again later and look at it more closely. If not, it will probably just go in the waste-paper basket.

Leaflets need to be on sturdy paper, as they often get rough treatment. The paper should be plain rather than glossy, so that people do not feel you are wasting money. If the leaflet is going to be folded – for instance, to go through a letter-box or into an envelope – design it so that it's clear what it is about, even when folded.

Keep one leaflet to one subject. If you have a continuing flow of stories to give people, turn your leaflets into a newsletter, with a standard 'look' (covered in Chapter 13).

Have a good headline. Keep it simple, and make it lead into the story you have to tell.

Give the words plenty of space. Separate out the important points, perhaps by using 'bullets' (like this, •), or by putting them in **bold** letters, a different-size typeface, or a shaded box. People will often be reading them 'on the run' so that the message has to be easy to take in.

Always put a contact address, the name and address of the printer, and a date on the leaflet, even if it is in very small print.

An example can be seen in Figure 11.1.

Figure 11.1

LET'S END TRAFFIC DANGER TO ELMBANK CHILDREN

Last week a 10-year-old boy was struck by a car on his way home from Elmbank School. Luckily, he escaped with cuts and bruises – but it could have been much worse.

The accident happened at the bend near the junction of Elmbank Road and Thistle Lane. It's known as an accident black spot. Five children have been injured there in the last few years. Now a group of parents has formed to campaign for new safety measures.

Cars come round that bend at 40 or 50 miles an hour, and there is no sign warning of a school ahead. There should be a sign before the bend. There should also be an island in the middle of the road. This would slow traffic down, and make crossing safer.

The Council has the money to do the work this year. But they need to be persuaded that it is urgently needed. A group of parents has already been to see them. We have now formed the Elmbank Action Campaign, to persuade all the other parents to show their concern.

If you support our campaign, fill in the form below and send it to our councillors at County Hall.

If you prefer, you could write your own letter to them. The address is ....
....

If you'd like to get involved in the campaign, contact the Secretary ....
....
....

To Councillors Errol, Maden, and Rushworth
I am a parent of .... children at Elmbank School. I support the campaign for the Council to build a traffic island on the bend by the junction of Elmbank Road and Thistle Lane, and to put up a School sign before it. The present situation is a danger to our children.

Signed (your name) ....

Printed and published by the Elmbank Action Campaign, c/o

Distribution

The more personal you can make the delivery of any leaflet, the fewer copies you will waste, and the greater the impact.

The best way to ensure that a leaflet is read by someone is to meet them face to face, get them interested, and then put it into their hands. The next best way is to deliver it to them in an envelope, individually addressed. As your distribution methods get more 'scatter-gun', the proportion of people who actually *read* the leaflet they are handed will get smaller and smaller. In a busy shopping centre on a Saturday morning perhaps one in ten or twenty will do so.

So you need more leaflets to make the same impact, or something else that is linked with them. You could for instance have an event, like a demonstration or the signing of a petition, or a street stall where people come and ask questions.

Concentrate your efforts on places where people will feel most personally involved in the issue. The campaign group in the example leaflet on page 118, for instance, should distribute its leaflet among parents at the school and people in the surrounding few streets (who also have to cross the dangerous road) rather than push leaflets through every letter box in town. Good 'targeting' saves money (and trees) because you need fewer leaflets. Always plan for some spares, though, for people who write in and enquire, and people who have forgotten they were ever sent one.

Addressing labels or envelopes is time-consuming, but worth it if you've got a limited list of identifiable people. You might, for instance, want to contact everyone on the electoral roll in half a dozen streets, or all of a community centre's membership.

Once the leaflets have been addressed, ask each of your helpers to deliver a certain number by a deadline. Ask them to return those they do not succeed with. There will always be some where there are fierce dogs lurking in gardens, for instance. Put a small element in your budget for posting these.

If you are not addressing your leaflets individually, ask a number of people each to take a bundle of leaflets, and a list of which streets they are to cover. Again, give them a deadline, and ask them to return any leaflets they can't deliver.

An alternative is to go out as a group, perhaps on a Sunday morning, and deliver everything at once. This tends to be more fun, and good for the morale of the group. Organise it so that pairs of people go up each street together, leapfrogging each other at alternate doors or on opposite sides of the street. The presence of another person will make your helpers feel braver about ringing all the bells in a block of flats with an entrance phone until they find someone to let them in.

Handing out leaflets in the street

Arrange for a group to work together, scattered round a junction or in a pedestrian area. You'll make more impact that way, and people will feel happier about doing the work if there are others around them. Leafleting in the street is depressing, because the majority of people pretend you don't exist, and walk straight past. Others take the leaflet and then drop it a few paces further on. This is mainly because they are busy people with other things on their minds, but it is difficult not to take it personally.

One person should be responsible for bringing the supplies of leaflets. If possible, provide also some badges or sashes for people to wear, so that they make more of a visual impact. There should be a definite meeting place, and a definite time at which to start and finish. Don't try leafleting in the pouring rain or bitter cold. People will not take leaflets then anyway.

Generally, you won't get much hassle if you are handing out leaflets that are uncontroversial or about a popular cause. You'll face more difficulties if the cause is controversial – there were problems for leafleters all through the miners' strike, for instance – or if you are combining the leaflet with a collection or a petition. You need formal permission for a collection. See *Organising Things* for details.

If the police ask you to move along, it's usually best to obey. Technically, you will generally be 'obstructing' by standing still in the middle of a busy pavement. Ask them where they would like you to stand, or find another spot yourselves and start again.

Shops often own the area immediately in front of their windows, so the managers are in their rights to ask you to move along. Indoor shopping malls generally belong to the development companies, who employ security guards to look after their property. It's rare for them to give permission for anyone to hand out leaflets. You are trespassing if you carry on once they have asked you to move.

Posters

These are useful for:

- Giving people basic information about an event – what's happening, when and where.
- Getting out a snappy message to reinforce the points being made more fully by other methods.
- Creating a mass display of support, visible to other members of the public and those taking the decision.
- Creating an image for your organisation or the campaign.

- Creating a commitment among the people who agree to display them. In politics, for instance, it's not easy to vote against someone when you have had their name in your window for the last three weeks.

Posters are not much use for getting across anything complicated or with a lot of details – the fewer words the better. There is an exception to this: in places where people are standing around with nothing to do, like the London Underground while waiting for a train, they will read long posters out of boredom. So think about where your posters will be sited *before* you start drawing them up.

Posters can be:

- Hand-drawn.
- Printed with a silkscreen.
- Produced on a computer and/or blown up to size with a photocopier.
- Professionally printed.

Hand-drawing is time consuming, and you need a skilled person to produce a good result. Most of the other possibilities are explained in Chapter 9 on printing techniques. Silkscreening is not covered, as it would take a lot of space and several pictures to do so. Look in Jonathan Zeitlyn's book (see Appendix 1: Booklist) for a good clear explanation. Amateurs who are good at craftwork can do it themselves, and it can give good results.

One possibility is to combine two methods: have a set of posters printed with your group's logo, and any permanent slogan, but leave enough space for the message, and then hand-draw that.

The message has to be brief, in short words, and self-explanatory. Vary the size of the print or use a different colour for the most important words.

Keep cartoons, drawings, or photos simple, and make sure that people can easily get the point.

Make sure your design fits in with the image you have already decided on. Don't be tempted to be brasher, or to use a slogan that is more aggressive, than you really want to be. Think carefully about the pictures you use. You might find something that is heart-rending, or very striking, but it has to get across the message you *intend* it to get across. Otherwise you are wasting your money, and might even be doing yourself positive harm.

The law

This is only a short summary: for more details look in *Organising Things*.

Posters count as advertisements in law, and so need planning permission from the local authority. They cannot normally object to the design and content of the poster, but only to where it is put. If your posters are going on a commercial hoarding or poster site, planning permission will have been given already for that site and you need not worry about seeking it again.

Posters advertising local non-commercial events of a 'religious, political, social, educational, cultural or recreational nature' and posters about parliamentary and local elections, do not need planning permission so long as:

– you have the permission of the site owner;
– the poster does not block or obscure the view of the road;
– it is no bigger than 0.6 metres square. Election posters can be bigger.

Hanging out banners is therefore technically illegal, as they will be bigger than this, but people are not often prosecuted for this.

A poster must not be put up more than 28 days before the event, and it must be taken down within a fortnight afterwards. This is a good idea anyway, as many people get irritated by seeing a lot of out of date material taking up space on walls or windows.

Tenants do not need the permission of their landlords to put up a poster. But they *might* be considered to be making a 'material change' to the fabric of the dwelling by nailing something to a wall. So if they say they do not want to take the risk, it's better not to press them.

Flyposting means putting up a poster without permission from the owner or the local authority. It is illegal, and the local authority has the power to remove or obliterate any flyposted material, though some are more active than others about doing so.

Every poster has to include a statement in small print about who has printed and published it, by law.

Announcing an event

The key points, for a poster announcing an event, are:

• Who is running it.
• What it is – for instance a jumble sale, a public meeting, a course.
• When it is being held – double check that you have included the time, the date *and* the day.
• Where it is being held. If it's not somewhere well-known, explain on the poster, or draw a map.

Getting them displayed

You can:

• Tie posters to lamp-posts, or put them on sticks in the hedgerows or in gardens. Stick them on cardboard first, and keep enough copies to replace those that are torn down or become unreadable because of sun or rain.

- Ask if you can put them up on the notice board in the local library, sports centre, community centre, or school, or the parish noticeboard in a village.
- Ask shopkeepers if you can put them in their window. They need to be fairly small, A3 or A4, for this.
- Ask if you can put them in launderettes and takeaways, and other places where people tend to wait around for a while.
- Ask your supporters to put copies in their windows.
- Flypost them on walls, bridges, etc (see page 122 for details of the law on this).

Concentrate on getting posters into places where they will be seen by the people who are likely to want to take part in the event. For a jumble sale, or a public meeting about a local issue, try to saturate the streets immediately around the venue – perhaps a dozen streets in each direction. For something with a wider appeal, concentrate on your main shopping streets, and the main library, community centre or sports centre, where the most people go. If you're in a country area, there will be a town that most people go to, but you should also try to get at least one poster into each village.

With libraries and community centres, there may be definite rules about how long a poster can stay up, what size it is, and what sort of events can be advertised.

Shopkeepers normally refuse to put up anything remotely controversial or political, especially party political. Your supporters may be wary also, if they feel that they might get a brick through their window. So you'll be left largely with flyposting.

Stress to everyone that you'd like the posters taken down immediately after the event.

Getting supporters to help

To get your supporters to put up a poster, make up packs with a couple of posters in each of them, and a friendly letter explaining what the point is, when they should put the poster up, and how long it should stay there for. Address the letter personally if possible. If you can, take it round to each of your supporters and knock on the door, or organise a party of people to do this.

Give each person the pack and explain what it's for. If they agree to put the poster up for you, ask whether they'd like you to put it in the window there and then. *Don't* pressure them on this, especially if they have never met you before. People are quite rightly worried by the idea of letting strangers into their house, and if you try the hard sell you could lose more supporters than you gain. But have some Sellotape or Blu-tack handy, and if they agree, put the poster up in the spot where it can be seen best from the road.

Do the same if you are putting them on sticks in gardens, or on any piece of land that definitely belongs to someone. You can probably get away without tracking down the farmer who owns the hedgerows along a main road, though.

Visiting shops and other places

Visiting shops, launderettes, pubs, supermarkets and similar places is best done in pairs. Many people find it an embarrassing and awkward task. You could get quite a number of refusals, which can be upsetting. With more than one person, you can compare notes and this will help you to take it less personally.

Go into the shop, or similar place, at a time when it is quiet. Wait your turn with the other customers, then produce your poster, explain what it is all about, and ask if it can go up. Say how long you will want it to stay up. Don't suggest too long a period, as people don't want to clutter their windows for weeks at a time. Stress that it is something local, or something that the customers are likely to be interested in.

The person on the counter may agree, or may say that s/he has no authority and that the manager or owner will have to decide. If you are going to have time to call back, find out when they will be around and make arrangements to return. Otherwise, leave the poster and ask for the message to be passed on.

Keep a note of the responses, distinguishing between the definite refusals and the, 'Well, I'll think about it,' comment. It's worth going back to those who are thinking about it, once a few other posters have gone up in the area. Once they realise that other people are doing it, and so it is not out of the way at all, those people could be happier.

National campaigns

If you are trying to arrange a national poster campaign, one possibility is to treat it as a series of local ones, and ask each group of your supporters to work through their area, in the ways described above.

Another method is to work through the post, sending each supporter a poster and an explanation of why you would like them to put it up. Or you could fold a copy of the poster into each copy of your regular magazine, and explain the reasons for it in an article.

These methods will not achieve a very high response, because people will feel isolated if they are the only ones in their area with a particular poster on show. But it is worth doing, for the sake of the brave or committed people. And even a low response rate will get you wider coverage than you could achieve in other ways.

Commercial billboard and poster sites

The other possibility is to advertise on billboard and poster sites. Some 'good causes' may be able to get these sites cheap, by approaching the major firms that rent them out and negotiating a discount. Those who don't count as good causes will have to pay full rates. This is expensive, but it is worth spending out a little *more* money going to a media buying agency who specialise in this, to make sure you have the right sites and the best deal possible. Find the agencies through PIMS or one of the media directories – see page 166. Give them a clear brief about what you want, and leave them to get on with it. The best – and therefore most expensive – sites are in busy shopping streets, on bus-routes, or near places like cinemas or bingo halls, where people may be queuing for a while. Poster Marketing (see Appendix 2: Addresses) can give you research figures about how many people pass by a particular site, and what sort of people they are.

Even if you are getting the sites cheap, or using your supporters to distribute the posters, a national poster campaign will still cost quite a lot. You *must* get the posters professionally designed and printed. You may be able to get the help of an advertising agency for free, or for less than commercial rates. Give them a careful brief. If after doing that the design turns out not to be suitable, say so. Don't let yourself feel guilty about 'looking a gift horse in the mouth.' You have probably been given the services of an inexperienced person, and the criticism will help him or her to learn.

Use the same agency to arrange for printing. The large posters on billboard sites are made up of a number of smaller sheets, and printing them correctly is a specialist job. It's also not cheap: for a national campaign you need about 1,600 posters, and that could cost £15,000 or more in printing costs.

Ask your supporters in different areas to monitor the sites, and tell you when the posters went up, how long they stayed, and whether the sites fitted your specifications. If they did not, and you had to pay for them, ask for a reduction on your bill.

You may be able to find sponsors who will help with the cost of a campaign of this sort, in return for having their logo printed on the poster beside yours.

Car stickers

It is best to think of a car sticker as a poster which moves. They are useful for:

– getting across a slogan; and
– showing support for a particular cause.

They are not good, though, at getting across detailed information, as most people will not have time to read them.

The wording of any car sticker should be self-explanatory. That means that anyone who sees the sticker for the first time should be able to grasp what it is about, even if they don't know the details of the issue. A straightforward statement of: 'Say Yes To ...' or 'Say No To ...' or 'Support ...' is best. If you can think up a wording that gets your point across, and is also clever and witty, that is a bonus.

Your design must be *readable* – with a clear logo, using capital letters. You must show which organisation is putting out the stickers. You can do this by using your logo, or by putting the name of the group in small letters beneath the slogan.

Car stickers can be printed on plastic with a peel-off surface. This would be too expensive, though, for most groups, and not worthwhile unless you were printing very large numbers. An alternative is to have them printed on paper, with gummed strips at each end. You will need to go through the same process of finding a printer and giving a specification as for a poster.

Distribution

Since each sticker is not expensive, and they are intended to help people show support, it makes sense to give most of them away rather than sell them. You could send them to all your supporters, or hand them out at meetings or other events. If you want to sell them, you could do this either by mail order (see Chapter 12) or by having a stall at various events and selling them along with other items such as reports and Christmas cards.

12

Pamphlets and reports

Reports and pamphlets about your work can be the foundation stones of your campaign. They can:

- Make public all the background material you have been working on, so that other people know what has brought you to think the way you do.
- Show the press, the politicians and others that you are trying to influence that you are serious, and know what you are talking about.
- Give you a reason to build newspaper and magazine contacts and stories, hold conferences and other events, and lobby people.

One group that bases much of its campaigning work around reports and pamphlets is Child Poverty Action Group (CPAG). They go to CPAG's own membership, and the group also manages to get considerable publicity, and exercise influence, through its publications. Their key point is their quality; they can be hard-hitting, but can also be relied on to be *accurate*, so that journalists can quote them without fear of being caught out.

Although this is a national group, it is equally possible for a local group to act in this way over an issue where they have built up special knowledge and expertise.

Pamphlets and reports can range in size from a thousand words or so (about three pages of this book), to the length of a short or even a long book. They can be very glossy with pictures and graphics, or typed and photocopied on plain paper and the paper stapled together, perhaps with a card cover.

The advantage of a pamphlet is that there is room to set out the evidence and show what you want done about it. But if done well, pamphlets can take considerable time and money to produce.

They are not ever likely to be read by large numbers of people. So it is important to make sure that they reach the *right* people, and to make the pamphlet attractive so that they will get around to reading it.

As with any other type of publication, you need to know before you start:

- what you are saying;
- to whom; and
- for what reason.

You also need to know why you are putting the material in a report or a pamphlet, rather than in something shorter or just in a press release.

Style

The rules of thumb set out in chapter 3 apply here as much as anywhere else. But there are some special points for this type of publication;

- Unless it's only a few pages long, divide your pamphlet into sections or chapters, each with a single main point. Put them in a logical order, so that it is easy to follow your argument. If you find that you must keep referring forward to something you have not yet said, the sections are almost certainly in the wrong order. Move them round until the arguments fit together. Getting the right structure for your pamphlet is the key to writing it properly and keeping it readable.

- Back up each statement with facts. Imagine you are talking to a particularly argumentative person, who is asking all the time, 'Who says?' and 'Where's your evidence?' So give the evidence *and its sources*. You might want to provide footnotes at the bottom of each page or the end of each chapter, but this is rather academic and can be offputting for people to read. You could instead say what the sources are as you go along, and then list them again at the end. Look at other pamphlets by people covering the same sort of issues as you are. What do they do, and what do you think would suit your readers best?

- If you do have points for which you can find no evidence, or opinions that you have formed as a result of looking at the facts, you can use a phrase like, 'Although it is not possible to prove this, it seems as if ... [children living in this part of the city have poorer health than those living where there are more parks]' or, 'One can infer that ... [the Education Committee would not be sorry if the school closed so that they could sell the site for housing.]' Don't try to present an opinion as a fact; you'll be caught out.

- If there are examples or statistics that point the other way, say so, and try to show why. Perhaps they are based on a very small sample, or the wrong people were asked, or the conditions in that case were too different to make a comparison possible.

- Don't expect your readers to concentrate for too long at a time, and make it easy for people to skim through your pamphlet and take in the main points. Many pamphlets these days have a summary at the beginning. This lists all the main points, and the conclusions and recommendations you have reached. It tells you which section deals with each of the main points.

At the beginning of each Chapter or section, you can also list the key points. Put these in **bold** or *italics* to make them stand out, or put a box round them.

If you have recommendations scattered through the different sections, collect them together and repeat them at the end. Do not bring in new material here, or in the conclusion.

- If you use statistics, include an explanation that ordinary people can understand. Many people don't understand graphs, and others don't like trying to take in facts from tables. Others, again, find them useful and easy to understand. So try to cater for everyone by giving an explanation in the text, as well as in the graph or table.
- Don't use algebra or complicated mathematical formulae. Most people gave up doing maths years before, and a page full of it is likely to frighten people off. If it's necessary at all, put an explanation alongside in clear English. You may need to explain the methods used in a survey or piece of research. But if it is technical, put it separately in an Appendix.

The title

Some organisations, such as Child Poverty Action Group, tend to go in for catchy titles with a pun in them – for instance, calling a report on debt and poverty 'Consuming Credit'. Others make the title more factual. There's no hard and fast rule, but points to remember are that:

- The main title should be short, and use short words. There can be an extra sentence, a sub-title, which can explain things more if you want.
- It helps if you make it easy to remember – perhaps by using a pun or having several words beginning with the same letter (called 'alliteration'), but it's more important to make it self-explanatory.
- The title should be decided *early,* not long after you've decided on the publication itself. This means that it can be used in advance publicity along with at least a rough sketch of the cover.

The cover
The design of your cover is crucial. You could compare it to the display in a shop window. If people are bored or repelled, they will look no further. If they are interested, they will pick up the book and turn over its pages, and hopefully get hooked. It's best, if you are a small group without an established reputation in publishing, not to be too experimental. Stay orthodox, but not dull.

Before you start thinking about the design you want, look round a few bookshops and see what is on the covers of other books or pamphlets that your readers might pick up. They need not be on the same subject – you'll be able to tell from your own experience, and any research you have done, what sort of topics are linked together by people's interests, so look at those too. People who are interested in politics, for instance, are likely to be interested in biographies, history and social sciences. Ask for advice in your local independent bookshop, or somewhere similar, about what seems to attract people.

The spine
One thing that makes a difference to whether a report or pamphlet can be sold in a bookshop or not, is whether it has a 'spine', that is, whether there is a flat end to the cover on which the title and author can be printed. In the bookshop, it will be standing on a shelf with this spine showing, and people will scan along the shelves looking at the various titles, deciding which to take out and look at more closely. If instead of a spine your report has two staples and a fold, people will not know what they are looking at, and so they will not take it out and thumb through it.

You can only put words on a spine if the pamphlet is thick enough, and it raises the cost of production, especially on a short print run, so you need to decide how important bookshop distribution is. Ask the printer for quotes on two alternative bases, stapled or with a spine, before you decide.

If you do have a spine, make sure the title is clear and can be read easily. Even without one, if the pamphlet is quite fat it will be worth getting a title printed on just beside the staples, so that it can be read on the bookshelf.

Distribution

Decide whether you are planning to sell your pamphlet or report, or to give it away. In many cases, the most economical method will be to arrange to give away free copies to those you want to influence, and to the press. Then you can just print that number, plus a few more for people who hear or read about it and are interested. If it turns out that in fact there is a much bigger demand than that, you can reprint. It will cost more per copy to have two fairly short runs rather than one long one, but your capital is not tied up in stocks waiting to be sold, and you can judge how many are needed with a fair chance of success.

Ask the printer for a quote for fewer than the number of copies you think you can realistically get rid of, and then ask also for the cost of reprinting an extra 500 or thousand copies. If you sell out but demand is fairly slow, you can do a small reprint. If it's brisk, you could instead update the text, and reprint with a different colour cover and the words 'Second edition' all over it. You might even get some of the people who have already bought the first edition coming back for more!

Pricing

Although you are giving most copies away, you can still put a price on the cover of your publication. Quote this in any news release or short leaflet about it, so that when people write in for a copy they enclose a cheque for the right amount. You can also sell it at conferences or courses. This will help to recoup the printing costs. Assume that you are unlikely to make a profit. Count your publication costs instead as part of the overall cost of the campaign.

Look round your local bookshop at the prices of other publications that could be compared with yours, then use this as a guide price for deciding what your feasible budget is. Commercial publishers 'mark up' the production costs (that is, multiply them) by five or six times to arrive at a cover price. This takes all the other costs into account – you should do the same.

You may want to do 'differential pricing'. That means you charge a different amount to different categories of people. So you could say that the unwaged paid £1, those with wages £5, and libraries, institutions and funded organisations £20, for instance. It is rather arbitrary and a few people will cheat, but most will be honest. Don't overdo this, though – you want it to be read, rather than profitable.

Marketing

This section is only a summary of the main points. For more detail, look in *Marketing for Small Publishers*, also published by Journeyman (see Appendix 1: Booklist for details).

Selling to a guaranteed market

One way to be able to publish larger numbers of copies, without too much risk, is to find a way of tying in with someone who can guarantee a certain number of sales. Or you can do this within your own organisation.

Child Poverty Action Group, for instance, includes the price of a certain number of pamphlets and books each year within its subscription rates, so that it knows that about 4,000 copies of each will go out automatically. It can then afford to print a few hundred extra, for distribution through other means, without taking too big a risk.

You might be able to get a special arrangement with a professional organisation, or someone organising a conference, to buy copies of your pamphlet or report in bulk. They will be especially attracted if they are getting *advance* copies. Often there are 'pre-publication offers' at a reduced price. Though this will reduce the income, it could be well worthwhile if it means you have the cash immediately to pay the printers' bills.

Mail order

This is probably the most sensible method for the group that is publishing pamphlets regularly or occasionally. Chapter 14, on letter writing, covers the points to think about in setting up a mailing list. For technical details about running a direct mail operation, there are several books listed in Appendix 1: Booklist.

To get orders in for a pamphlet you are selling in this way, you will need to make sure that people know it exists. This means that you need:

- A good leaflet, distributed as widely as possible to people you think will be interested. See Chapter 11 on how to put together and distribute a leaflet.
- Good press and media coverage, in places where interested people are likely to see it. A feature article would be especially valuable, if you can persuade an editor to do one. A small mention in the 'Noticeboard' section of a paper or magazine is also useful. Reviews are helpful, even if they are not too friendly, so long as they do not damn it completely. See Chapters 16 and 17 for details of how to get media coverage.

Advertisements can also be worthwhile, but are best in conjunction with other publicity. They are too difficult to 'target' accurately to be worth using on their own. See Chapter 19 for more on this.

If you are planning mail order sales, it is essential to build in the time to do them properly. You need to keep careful records of the orders and the money, and to send out your copies in response as quickly as you can. If you don't do this, you will lose by having a reputation for sloppiness at least as much as you will gain by publishing something good.

Selling through bookshops

This is fairly difficult and time-consuming. The number of radical bookshops, and their sales, are both declining. Their place is being taken by the chains like Waterstones and Dillons.

To sell in bookshops, you need to start by persuading the person who runs the bookshop that the customer will be interested. There are various ways of making contact.

One is 'do-it-yourself' – the author, or the group, actually going round bookshops selling copies to the person running the shop. If it's a local publication, perhaps a local history or a collection of short stories or reminiscences from people in a particular area, you might be able to persuade other shops besides bookshops to take copies. Newsagents and gift shops, for instance, might be interested. Even pubs have been known to put a few copies behind the bar.

Concentrate on the small family or single-owner shops, rather than the chains. The big firms of booksellers give their local managers very little discretion about what they can order locally. In some cases, the local manager will have power to buy, but not to make any payments, as these have to go through the central accounts department. There will be special controls on setting up new accounts with unknown firms.

You can sell to bookshops in three different ways. It is essential to know which you are doing at any one time. They are:

- Firm sale: the book is bought and paid for by the bookseller, and they can't return it even if it doesn't sell.

- Sale or return: the book is bought and paid for, but can be returned without prior arrangement, and you then need to pay the money back.

- Consignment: the book is only paid for when it's been sold. The bookseller keeps it for as long as s/he things fit, and then returns unsold copies at any time.

You're unlikely to achieve a firm sale as a small publisher. It's far more likely to be sale or return or consignment.

Keep a good record of who has got what, on what terms, and what they owe you, and then pursue them for the money and further orders. Ask anyone who is holding stocks of books on your behalf to sign a receipt or some other form when he or she takes them, so that you have evidence of how many they have had, when, and how much you were expecting to be paid for them.

You sell to bookshops at less than the cover price, because they expect a 'mark-up' for their trouble. Normally, you'll need to give a discount of about one-third of the price. So if you were asking them to sell something for £3, you'd only get £2 per copy.

You are only likely to get repeat orders if:

- the report or pamphlet has sold well; and
- you go back again, or make contact on the phone, and use all your powers of persuasion.

Even then, many people will feel they have done their bit and do not want to be bothered any more.

Distributors

These are the firms who will store stocks of books in their warehouses, send out orders and invoice people for the money. They then pass on what they collect to you, less a percentage to cover their costs. Most of the large distributors and some of the small ones will only take on work for publishers who are going to give them a steady stream of work, not for organisations that publish something once in a blue moon.

'Full Service', including 'repping' (explained in the next section) is likely to take 55 per cent of your cover price. That is, if the price of the book in the shop is £3, the distributor gets £1.65 and the publisher £1.35.

'Repping'

This is short for 'representation' and it means the task of persuading the bookseller that he or she wants to take copies of your report or pamphlet and display it on the shelves. The main sales push is done before the book is published, and the representative can't therefore take books themselves round. Instead he or she makes up a file of 'Advance information sheets', so when the bookseller is looking at details of your publication, he or she is looking also at the details of perhaps 50 or 100 other publications at the same time, on all sorts of different subjects. He or she has to be convinced that yours will sell.

Advance information (AI) sheets

These give details in a standard form of the title, the author, the price, the publication date and what it is about.

The wording of the 'blurb' is very important; it is all that the bookseller has got when he or she is trying to judge whether to take the book or not. It needs to be concise, and make selling points. For instance, it must cover what audience is likely to be attracted, whether it is topical, whether there are other books in the field, what plans there are for publicity. If you are going to issue news releases, and may be getting radio or TV publicity, stress the fact.

Anything by a well-known publisher or author starts at an immediate advantage. If your organisation or author are not well-known, try to find someone who is, to help out. They could write a foreword, or a conclusion, or send you a quote to put on the back or the front of the book saying how wonderful it is.

The other important item for the rep is a copy of the book's jacket or cover. If this is not ready, then a good reproduction of the artwork, or even a line drawing showing what it is expected to look like, will help. You can get colour Xerox copies of drawings or photographs today, which look almost the same as the original.

Directories and bibliographies

If you get publicity for your report, people may well enquire about it in their local bookshop. To order it, they will need to be able to track it down, and for this it needs to be in at least one of the main lists, such as *British Books in Print*.

To get into this, the first step is to be allocated an International Standard Book Number (ISBN). This is the number you'll see on the page opposite the title page in almost every book. The Standard Book Numbering Agency (12 Dyott Street, London WC1A 1DF) arranges these, and you can send for a form to fill in. There is a fee, but it is not high and is well worthwhile.

For details of how to get into the bibliographies and lists, once you have your ISBN, see *Marketing for Small Publishers* (see Appendix 1: Booklist).

Libraries

Libraries prefer hard-back books to paperbacks or pamphlets, but may be interested in your report if it is topical or about the local area. Usually the libraries buy most of their books through big suppliers, but many also have a policy of ordering some material through local bookshops.

It's worth sending copies of the AI sheets to all the library suppliers listed in *Marketing for Small Publishers*. If your report is of local interest, it will also be worth going into the main library and any branch libraries with a copy of the AI sheet, and asking to see the senior person. They might be willing to put up a display for you when it is published, though this is unlikely if it is controversial.

What else to do with your report

Chapter 17 explains how to produce news releases about reports or pamphlets, so that they become 'stories' for the media.

You might also want to use a shortened version as an article in your newsletter or magazine, or as a leaflet. It will anyway always be worth advertising the pamphlet there, even if it has already gone out to the members. People who have only just started to get interested will not have received it, and could want to send off for it.

13

Magazines and newsletters

Magazines and newsletters can be single page leaflets, or a few pages folded together, or a large fold-out sheet designed to look like a newspaper. Or they can have 20 or 40 pages and be stapled together or bound with glue.

For convenience, this chapter describes them all as magazines, though you may call your own version:

- a newsletter
- a bulletin
- a magazine; or
- a journal.

Magazines are useful for:

- Keeping members of the group in touch with each other.
- Giving information about the progress of different aspects of the campaign.
- Keeping supporters up to date with research that has been going on, or new facts that have emerged.
- Giving news about the campaign to those outside the group, perhaps in the local area, so that they know what is happening and can feel involved even if they are not active.
- Introducing the group to other people. Often if someone enquires about your campaign, the most practical thing to send them is a copy of your magazine. This will let them know who you are, and give them the 'flavour' of the group.

They will often be kept and filed, and looked at again later when people want to check a fact, or see what was happening at a particular time. They will also be read from cover to cover in many cases, since they will mainly be going to supporters or people who are thinking of becoming supporters. They are very important to the image of the organisation – in a way, they are its permanent 'shop window' to the world.

Once you call something a magazine, you've committed yourself to producing a series in a particular format, whereas a pamphlet is a one-off. So you should not start one without serious thought. It is a major commitment for a group, and it could be a millstone round your neck, stopping you doing other things you are more interested in. Be realistic about how regularly it is going to come out. Tell the readers, and then stick to it. It's better to *say* you'll be publishing every four months and do so, than to tell people you'll be publishing every three months and in fact be a month late each time.

Write each article in your magazine with the new reader in mind, rather than the old hand who knows it all. Even though you are producing a series, there will be newcomers each time, and some people who threw away the last edition but are now interested.

Layout and design

Make your design a *unity*, so that people know what magazine they are reading, all the way through. You can do this for instance by having 'straplines' – blocks of colour or a background tint with a subject heading on them, as in Figure 13.1, for example, at the top or bottom

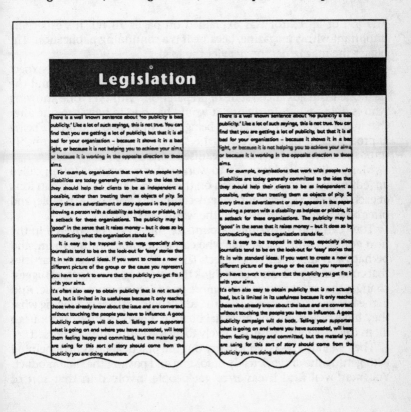

of each page. You could also have the headlines in the same typeface – though varying the sizes – all the way through, and use the same sort of grid for your layout on each page. See Chapters 8 and 9 for explanations of layout and printing methods.

Don't try to put too much in. Decide which stories are the most important or most interesting, and give them the full length. Cut the less important ones down to the single sentences that summarise them, and put them in a 'Newspoints' section on one page. Look at a newspaper to see how they do this.

Make it clear where each article begins and ends. Try to keep each article together, rather than 'continued on page 10,' so that it is easy to read. Vary the stories in length, with a few little snippets that people can glance at quickly. Don't make any of them too long. The average article in a 'quality' newspaper (explained on page 163) is about 800 words; in a serious magazine it would be rather longer, perhaps 1,500 or 2,000 words. Keep yours well within these limits.

Advance planning

The job of an editor was explained on pages 78–80. It's especially important with a magazine, because it is a continuing publication. The bigger the magazine, the heavier the load.

The editor needs to work out a planning cycle. You should expect to have one edition at the printers or just being distributed, and the next one in an advanced state of preparation, with everyone knowing who is doing what. In theory, it would be good to have the one after that under discussion, with ideas being thrown around and people being approached to write pieces, at the same time. But that is probably impossible even for the best organised editor.

Many editors find it useful to work with a committee (often called an 'editorial board') rather than on their own. The members can look at each edition, take account of any comments from other people, and offer constructive criticisms of the words and design.

They can also throw ideas around for subjects to be covered in the next editions, think of people who can write and illustrate them, and perhaps also approach them direct. They will be able to read the articles that come in, say whether they think they are good enough, and suggest changes that might make them more up to date or more readable. And in the last resort, if someone lets the editor down by not producing what they have promised, the editorial board is a ready source of labour to fill in the gap. Otherwise, it's likely to be the editor him- or herself.

They can also be asked to carry out the practical tasks, like helping with getting the artwork ready or folding and posting the final product. You may well find it easier to get people involved in that sort of practical work, if they know that they can also take part in creating the magazine itself.

It's usually best if the editor has the final say, rather than the board, however, because of the speed at which things can change. The organisation still has control, though, if the main committee has the power to sack the editor.

There should be a meeting of the editorial board as often as there is an edition of the magazine. If there are practical tasks to be done, you may need two meetings – one for those tasks, the other for discussing what is to be in the magazine.

Filling the magazine

Aim to have more than enough material to go into each edition. It is easier to cut an article, or to shorten it, than it is to produce one out of thin air at the last minute. But don't commission so much work that you have a lot left over at the end. People get upset if their work isn't used, or is held over from one edition to the next.

To plan a short magazine of say, four or eight pages, the simplest method is to draw a picture of each page, divided into columns if you are using them, and write in each space the title of the piece you are using, as in the example on page 140. You can also draw in a space for photographs or drawings (see Figure 13.2).

For a long magazine, draw up a list of what's to go on each page, like the contents page that will go at the front.

It's helpful to the readers, and to the editor, if there are certain regular slots in which the same type of article goes each time, like 'News Shorts' or 'Personal View'. A mixture of about half regular features, half one-offs, is probably about right. Each edition needs one *main* article, either covering an important story, or written by someone important, or both.

What goes at the front

The front page – whether it is a separate cover or part of the magazine with articles in it – is very important. It will catch the eye first, and may be what persuades the average person to pick the magazine up or not to bother. It needs to 'sell' the magazine, and the organisation, effectively. If you have articles on the front page, think particularly about the headline for the main story, and the overall image the page conveys. Does it look interesting, well put together and as if someone cares? Or does it give the impression of being boring, untidy, and thrown together in a hurry?

Your front page will need:

- a 'masthead' which tells people what the newsletter is, who is publishing it, and when;
- a striking headline which gets across the message you are trying to convey, preferably in a positive way; and
- an eye catching picture or drawing which adds to that message.

Figure 13.2

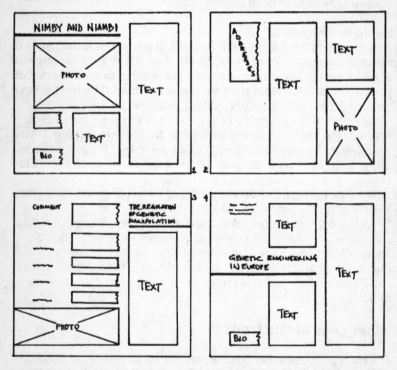

The first sentence of your main story will decide, for many people, whether they should read the rest of the newsletter or not. So it's worth thinking hard about which story should be the main one, and about what the point of it is. Chapter 17 explains what makes a story 'newsworthy'. Try to make sure that your main story does fit in with these ideas, as it is what the public will tend to expect as well.

For a magazine with a separate outside cover, again it is worth spending some time, and perhaps also money, on the design. You could use a striking photograph or drawing each time. Try to relate it to one of the stories inside, preferably the main one. If you have a 'name' writing for you or being interviewed, put the fact on the front cover, in as few words as possible. Look at commercial magazines to see how they do this. Make sure that the words are readable but do not obscure the picture.

Unless you can think of a very striking name, stick to something simple that explains itself. *Poverty*, for instance, is the name of CPAG's magazine, and *Roof* that of Shelter. Check (in BRAD, or PIMS Media Guide, see page 166) that no one else is using that title, otherwise you could be breaking their copyright.

Number and date each edition. Put on a realistic date for when you are publishing – later rather than earlier. It is annoying to be sent something which says that it is the October edition in November.

Use the same style each time, so that people can see that the magazine is part of a series. Print a 'logo' (a symbol for your organisation) on the cover, and at the top of the first page of each edition.

Use the back cover to advertise your own group's activities or publications, so that people get an impression of you even if the magazine is face downwards.

The editorial

If your magazine is more than a few pages long, the first page should have a table of contents and, running along side it, an 'editorial'. This is often written by the editor, but it could be written instead by the head of the organisation.

Decide early in the planning for each edition whose turn it is this time, but hold up the actual writing until a late stage, so that it can be topical. When the time comes, however, you need to take even more care with it than with any other article – because more people will read it than anything else. If your organisation is declaring its policy, this is the place for it. Anything that is said here is likely to be taken as policy, so you may need to arrange to check the editorial over quickly with the right people before it goes to the printer.

Advertising

One way to pay your publishing costs is to take advertisements in the magazine. Small local groups with photocopied or duplicated newsletters should be able to persuade local shops or businesses to take advertising space, as a gesture of goodwill, even though the publication does not look very professional. In general, though, it will only be possible to obtain advertising on a large scale if your magazine is printed, looks professional, and has a readership of at least two or three thousand.

Getting advertisements takes up considerable time. You'd probably need to employ someone almost full-time for a serious magazine to pay its way through advertising. Work out the costs carefully, and see how much profit you will actually make by selling advertising. If it means increasing the size of the magazine, this will increase your printing and layout costs, and also the postage to subscribers. Your editor will also have to find extra copy to fill the space between the advertisements.

There could also be other implications for your image. Will it make people think of you as commercial, for instance? Or will it add to your credibility because your readers will see that others are willing to pay for space in the magazine? Are there any types of advertisements that you would have to refuse, because they would cast doubt on your good faith? An example would be tobacco advertisements in a cancer charity's magazine.

Be careful about accepting advertising by anyone who you might want to oppose or to influence in the future. If you publish an article critical of an advertiser, they are likely to refuse to advertise in the magazine again. If you have become dependent on them, there will be an unconscious pressure to limit what you say.

Charging for the advertisements

Magazines that take regular advertising print 'rate-cards' – postcard-sized cards or a simple A4 sheet of paper, giving details of circulation and target groups, the price per page, half- and quarter-page, any special considerations, the deadline for advertising for each edition, and a name or phone number to contact.

Alternatively, you can print these details on one page of the magazine itself, and send a photocopy of that panel to anyone enquiring.

To work out what to charge, get the rate cards for a few magazines with similar circulations and targeted at the same people. Price yourself comparably: charging at less than commercial rates will not help you to get advertisements, as the potential advertisers will be suspicious of your quality.

Types of advertising you could look for are:

- Advertisements from publishers about books and publications, and by people producing materials or equipment your readers might be interested in.

- Advertisements by other groups and organisations about forth-coming meetings, conferences and similar events. These other groups could well be people working in competition with you. Develop a policy about what you want advertised, and what you do not.

- 'Solidarity' advertisements by organisations that want to give you their support. Trade union branches and regions, for instance, often take advertisements in *Labour Research*.

- Job advertisements, if your magazine comes out frequently enough. This is only really possible for one that is published at least monthly.

Decide how many pages of the magazine you want to hand over to advertising, and which pages you will use in this way. Commercial publishers find that they need somewhere between 50 and 60 per cent of their pages to be 'copy' – that is articles or news stories – to keep their readers. For a voluntary or campaigning organisation, it's probably more like two pages of copy to every page of advertising.

You can also take 'inserts' – leaflets that are folded in with the magazine. There should not be more than three in each issue, otherwise your readers will become irritated at the shower of paper dropping out of the magazine. If you are paying for the mailing to be done (see below) putting in inserts will cost extra. It will also add to the cost of postage. Allow for this when deciding whether to try to get this work.

The advertising manager

One person should take on the role of advertising manager, with help if necessary. The main tasks are:

- Assembling a list of the organisations that are worth contacting to see if they are interested in advertising. This means going through the various directories (in a big reference library or business library) to get together a set of addresses.

- Writing to them saying what is available, what the prices, specifications and deadlines are. Look in Chapter 14, on direct mail, for some ideas on how to write letters of this sort.

- Following up those who don't respond, with a phone call or another letter.

- Sorting out what those who are interested actually want to do, and getting the artwork (explained on page 92) ready for the printer. You can say that you want all your advertisements in camera-ready form, but you'll get a better response if you accept draft copy and have it typeset with your own material, according to their specifications. They will expect to pay a little extra for this. With inserts, the advertisers are expected to produce the complete final version, in the right quantities at the right time, so your task is to pressure them into doing so.

After publication, the advertising manager must send copies of the advertisements to the advertisers, with an invoice for the cost, and chase them up if they haven't paid.

There will also be negotiations with people who want their advertisements in a particular place, or a special financial deal. People may want swap arrangements where neither side pays anything, and each advertises in the other's magazine. These are worthwhile, as long as the group concerned is one with whom you'd be happy to advertise anyway. There is an opportunity cost to a swap of this sort – you could be turning away someone who wants to pay for the same space.

Distribution

The easiest method of distribution is to your supporters. A locally based group can arrange for a network of deliverers, each of whom will drop the magazine in at, say, 20 addresses. Let them know when it will be ready, and ask them to come and pick it up if possible. So that the magazine is not out of date by the time it reaches the readers, give them a definite deadline by which the task should be done.

If possible, each deliverer should be asked to knock on the doors, and have a word with the member or supporter before handing over the magazine. This means that everyone is kept in touch with the organisation on a regular basis. It will allow people to pass on ideas, comments about the group, or grumbles.

For a larger organisation, or one that is geographically spread out, you'll have to rely on the post. This means setting up a regular arrangement for people to help with addressing and filling envelopes. Get as many people involved as possible. It could tie up the time of your committee, or paid staff, for a considerable part of each month if it is left to them.

Computerise your mailing list, or put it on sheets from which you can copy sticky labels, as soon as you can. Ways of doing this, and of keeping the list up to date, are discussed on page 148.

If your subscription list is large – a thousand or more – it will be worth going to a mailing house to do the work for you. Though it is not cheap, the time saved by the people who are running the organisation is probably worth more. You will need to be rigorous about deadlines, and about the weight of each package.

For a smaller operation, there are special offers from Post Office Business Services which can help cut the cost and the effort. If you are posting more than 120 identical items, the Post Office will accept counted bundles at their sorting offices, and frank them mechanically at no extra cost. At sub post offices, they will accept bundles of 500 identical ones. You can also buy packs of 100 pre-paid envelopes. The address of your local Post Office Business Services will be in the phone book.

Other points about distribution

Think about your subscription levels. You might want to allow people to subscribe just for your magazine, without paying part of the general running costs of the organisation. Corporate bodies, like libraries and universities, often find this useful. It's possible also to have a *higher* subscription for them than for individuals, given that far more people will be reading their copies.

Although your subscribers or members will be the main market for the magazine, it's worth printing some extras each time, to send out to new supporters, or to put on the bookstall at a conference.

Selling magazines to bookshops and newsagents is even more difficult than selling books and pamphlets to them. The large distributors, like W H Smith's, really control the network, and it is hard to break in without a considerable amount of capital.

However, a local group with support in the area can set up its own network. This would mean visiting the shops each time there is a new issue, taking the money from the last one, and taking back unsold copies, then giving a fresh supply to the shopkeeper. It takes quite a lot of work, though, and you do need to be *reliable*.

Spin offs

You can make extra use of the main stories in your magazine by issuing a news release about them to newspapers or other media who are likely to be interested – see Chapter 17 for details of how to do this. Send the news release, plus a copy of the complete magazine, a few days in advance of the publication date with an embargo on it (see page 183). This gives the reporter time to read the story and do any follow-up work that's needed. You might be able to persuade the editor to reprint all or part of a good story, if you already have good contacts with him or her.

You can also produce 'off-prints' – separate printed or photocopied copies – of important articles, and send them out separately.

14

Letter writing

Writing letters, on a small or large scale, is a highly effective method of communication. This is because a letter is personal. It's the written or printed equivalent of a face-to-face conversation.

People like to receive letters, will read them, often more than once, and frequently respond. You can use letters for:

- Contacting existing supporters to ask them for money, or other forms of help such as lobbying politicians on your behalf.
- Contacting people who have expressed an interest in what you are doing, or in activities like yours, and asking them to join you or send you money.
- Contacting new groups, with the hope of getting them to become supporters, or to buy things that you sell.

The most usual name for this sort of activity is direct mail, so it will be called that in the rest of this chapter.

Who to write to

Direct mail is 'targeted' at particular people, and you can be pretty sure that it is at least glanced at. Very few people can leave a letter unopened, even if they think they know what is inside. And once it is open, most people will at least glance at it, and many will read it with care. So, rather than the random approach of advertising and leaflets, you can direct your efforts at those whom you really want to read the material – if you can find them.

However, getting the message to them is expensive, even with the special deals that can be arranged through Post Office Business Services. The cost of postage, printing and design, along with the labour costs of getting ready for a big mailing and dealing with the results, means that you could be talking about more than £1 for each address to which you mail. So you need to make sure that they go to the addresses where you are most likely to get a favourable response.

Your best response will usually come from people who already support you. After that will come people who support other groups or organisations like you, or who are likely to have a special need or desire for what you produce. So for instance, the playscheme association used as an example in Chapter 6 would probably get a reasonable response from parents of school age children in the area where they were running schemes. A Third World charity would get a response from people already supporting Third World groups.

In the commercial world, the statistics are that if you are mailing 'cold' to a completely new group, you're lucky to get a 3 per cent response rate. With a group who already know you, and have bought something from you in the past, the rate can climb to 10 per cent or more. With loyal supporters, it could be as high as 25 per cent – though it will drop off if people begin to feel you are asking too much of them.

Responses come in immediately if the mailing is going to be successful, but can also be followed up over a long period of time, by people who have been thinking about their purchase, or trying to get the money together. The response rate to mailings to the same group tends to follow a curved pattern. It rises over six or seven repeat mailings, then gradually falls away, unless you have something new or special to offer.

To build up a mailing list for the future, you need a record of virtually every name and address that comes into the office. This could include people who:

- Write in to offer their support, or to ask for information, or to buy something that you have for sale.

- Sign your attendance sheet or supporters' list at a meeting, or when you are running an event or a stall in the high street on a Saturday.

- Answer an advertisement you put in the local or national papers, or respond to a radio or TV appeal, or contact you after a story has appeared in one of the media.

With a self help group, such as an association concerned with a particular disease, the whole future of the organisation depends on its ability to turn people who come with problems into active campaigners. So they should also follow up anyone who comes for help, unless they state clearly that they don't want to be contacted again.

On the other hand, it would be wrong for a group like Child Poverty Action Group, that works on behalf of social security claimants, to send fundraising appeals to those claimants, after answering their queries. In any case, it would not work because those claimants simply do not have the money. But there are also a lot of better off professionals who use CPAG's services and buy its books. They can be tapped for money that can then be used to help the poor.

Be wary of using signatures that you have collected from petitions. People are very touchy about this; they don't feel that their names ought to be collected for one purpose and used for another.

It's possible to borrow other organisations' mailing lists, or rent them from commercial organisations. But it is liable to be an expensive exercise, so you need to be sure that the list you are using is the right one. This would usually mean testing it (explained below).

Any mailing list needs to be 'clean', that is, you need to have as few addresses as possible on it that are out of date, or duplicates of others, or belonging to people who have been written to many times and not responded. Having addresses of this sort on your list is a waste of resources. It is also likely to irritate people who find themselves receiving the same letter two or three times over, or continually redirecting mail to the person who moved out three years ago.

Creating and maintaining a system

For a small group with limited resources, putting together a mailing list might mean setting up a card index with the necessary information on it. But if possible, it's worth investing in a computer – or space on someone else's – with a good database package that allows you to sort the addresses in different ways, and to store extra information about the way in which you recruited them to the mailing list, and the responses you have had. The Community Computing network, explained on page 97, or a consultant, should be able to help you with buying the right software.

Once you have set the system up, then each time a query is answered, or an order is met, the name and address should go into your system along with a record of why it is there. You should be able to use the information in other ways as well – for instance, to help manage the workflow by seeing what the level of demand is, and where it is coming from.

If you are keeping your list on a computer, you may well need to register with the Data Protection Registrar. There are exemptions, but they are extremely limited, and you will probably find you are not covered by them if you are using your database for anything except a straight list of names and addresses. To find out more, and to get advice on whether you should register or not, contact the Registrar (see Appendix 2: Addresses).

Testing your list
Commercial firms are always advised to *test* their lists, using a sample big enough to be statistically valid. This is good advice, but it may not always be possible for a small group or a small mailing. If you are asking for support rather than money – for instance, for people to write

letters to their MPs about an issue – a test mailing will anyway not tell you very much, because you won't be able to find out what the response has been.

However, if you are asking for money, or for people to buy your publications or other products, it is sensible to do a pilot run, to see what response you are likely to get. Work out a budget, and see what level of response would make a difference between success and failure. Then ask someone who understands statistics to work out what proportion of your total mailing you need to test. The smaller the sample, the greater the margin of error – that is, the chance that your results will be wrong. Take this into account when deciding whether to go ahead or not.

If you are pinning a lot of hopes on the mailing – for instance, if the whole of your fund-raising strategy is based on it – testing is vital. You may even need to find a market researcher to design and run a proper study.

Groups that are trying to finance themselves, but are not charities, may be able to get DTI or local authority money to do some market research. AA Enterprises, for instance, the marketing arm of Anti-Apartheid, was able to do this a few years ago.

The grants available vary at different times and different places. Ask your local council's Economic Development Unit, or a small business advice centre, about the possibilities.

It is against the law to try to sell something that does not exist, and that you do not intend to produce. So if you send a letter inviting people to buy something, you are committed to producing it – at least in some quantities – whatever the response to your test. The best way round this is to say in your letter or leaflet that this *is* a test mailing, and that if production goes ahead, they will then be asked for money. If you have other items for sale, you could offer them at the same time.

There are other ways in which you could test your guesses about which other groups would be sympathetic to you, without having to prepare a mailing. One is to put an advertisement, or an insert, in the other group's magazine and see what response you get. This would not be statistically sound, but it would give you a good idea about whether or not people were sympathetic. If the response was very poor, you could drop the idea; if it was reasonable, you could go ahead with a test mailing before doing a complete one.

Style and content

The commercial firms that specialise in direct mailing have developed a particular style of letter writing for this. They say that it is used because of the evidence that it works. Alternatively, people may be so used to it that other styles would not strike them as being direct mail at all, so they would not know what to do with it.

Look at a direct mail letter next time you are sent one. You'll see that the style is:

- chatty – usually written as if the person had buttonholed you and was talking earnestly face-to-face;
- personal – working in references to you as an individual wherever possible, often including anecdotes and examples to which you are likely to relate; and
- wordy – many run into three or four pages of text.

Making the letter chatty and personal is certainly important. Although your group may be sending out several hundred or thousand of these, each individual will be reading it privately, in his or her home over the breakfast table or when just back from work.

It's not necessary, though, to make the letter as long as many are. A short one will save cost and paper. If you have a lot to say that's relevant, though, direct mail does give you a chance to say it all. But you still need to make every word count. People will lose interest if you are too verbose. Imagine while you are drafting it that you are talking to them, and that they can wander away if they are bored.

The convention is to emphasise major points by underlining words, or whole sentences, or by indenting paragraphs. That does seem to work, but don't go to excess. Keep the layout clear and uncluttered.

The first sentence has to attract him or her, if the letter is not to go straight in the bin. It could be an explanation of why the person is being written to at all. For example, someone fund-raising for a women's group among like-minded friends and contacts might want to start like this:

> I am writing to you because I know you are concerned about women's situation in this country, and have had to fight some tough battles in the past over women's issues.

Alternatively, your first sentence could have 'gut-appeal'. A recent appeal letter from Save the Children, for instance, began:

> Sadly, it's true. Every day children die because they haven't been given a simple vaccination against diseases like TB, measles, whooping cough, diptheria and tetanus. Diseases that, as you know, our own children are vaccinated against as a matter of course.

When deciding on what should go out, weigh a sample envelope, label and letter and calculate the postage. If you can do it without moving up into a higher cost-band, it makes sense to take the opportunity to include other pieces of material – such as a leaflet or prepaid envelope. Again, the professionals say that both of these include the response rate.

Dealing with responses

When you prepare for a big mailing, plan also for dealing with the responses. This will affect your image as an organisation as much as the initial mailing. Aim to react quickly and efficiently, on such things as:

- Sending receipts for donations.
- Sending out membership cards and publications.
- Following up requests for further information or queries about your work.

Responding quickly may involve staff dropping other pieces of work, or volunteers giving extra time. Try to work out, in advance, how much time dealing with each response will take, and how it will be done. Then think about both what level of response you can expect, and what response you *might* have if things went very well. You might, for instance, want to assume a 10 per cent expected response, but a 25 per cent 'optimistic' one. Plan how you would handle this optimistic one. Who could you ask to help, or what other work could be postponed? If there is no way in which you could handle it, scale down your mailing rather than disappoint or annoy people by a long delay after they have written to you.

Try to record information about everyone who responds, on your card index or computer, for future use. That will then give you the basis of your list for your next mailing.

15

Producing videos and tapes

Many campaigning groups and trade unions are attracted by the idea of using videos to get their message across.

The tapes themselves are now cheap, especially if bought in bulk, and video machines are increasingly common. *But* there are several important points to think about, before you decide to get involved:

- Making a video to a good standard is extremely expensive – *at least* £1,000 a minute is likely, or more if you are moving a camera crew around.

- This is because we are used to very high technical standards on TV, and won't tolerate anything else. That means good equipment, and skilled editing and production.

- Each audience for showing a video is small. If you're using a domestic screen, the maximum is about ten. For a large screen at a conference or education centre, perhaps 30 people can watch comfortably.

Taken together, these points mean that for it to be worthwhile, you need to be clear before you start *exactly* why you are making a video, who it is for, how it will be distributed, when and where it will be seen, and what it is meant to achieve. There are plenty of stories of organisations who decide to 'make a video' and end up with copies sitting on their shelves as expensive ornaments.

Advantages of video

Video does have some major advantages:

- Many people do not want to read much, and are used to getting their information from the television. So they may be more willing to watch a video than they would be to read one of your leaflets or come to a meeting.

- If it is well done, the individual feels that the presenter is talking to him or her personally. So you can achieve almost as much as talking to people face to face. As explained in Chapter 4, this is about the most powerful method of communication around.

• You can ensure that the message is being explained in exactly the same way each time, whereas when you are talking face to face it will vary.

• You can get over a message, even a fairly complex one, in a way which sticks in people's minds. You can reinforce words with pictures, and have different voices putting different parts of the argument.

So video works best, first, when you want to brief your own members or supporters about a change, or an event, getting over the arguments to a particular group in a controlled way. The UCW and some of the Civil Service unions, for instance, have used it to get over the details of agreements.

Second, it's useful for training purposes, for example when you want to send one group of people out to talk to others, perhaps in a recruiting drive or when canvassing for votes. It can give them a real 'feel' for what they will be doing. The TUC, for instance, prepared two videos as part of their briefing material during the campaigns for a Yes vote on the Political Fund ballots, to help activists think about the arguments that would work best with their ordinary members. Here, the video was backing up other material such as leaflets and briefing packs, showing how they would be used and what reaction people might get.

Video is also helpful for new recruits to your group or your campaign, or those who have just started working at your place. You can give them a video that explains who you are and what you do, in the form of a 'one-to-one' talk, that they can play over at a time convenient to themselves.

Videos are not very good at taking people through a very detailed argument, or giving them a mass of facts. But they can give the broad outlines, and tie in with leaflets, booklets, or circulars which give the details. *Interactive* video is even more expensive than the ordinary sort, but it allows people to ask questions or test their knowledge through the machine, which makes it a good learning method. When the price comes down, it will be an excellent way to take people through arguments or methods of working.

People are used to TV programmes being made a certain way, and programmes need to fit in with these conventions to be acceptable. For example, most programme makers assume that people's attention slips after three minutes at most, so that they must then change the subject or change the approach. If this was not true to start with, it probably is now. People will be bored if your programme keeps to one subject or one approach for much longer than that. People are also used to 'balanced' discussions, and to interviewers who put the opposite side of the case. If you don't provide these, they could accuse you of being biased.

Shelf life

A good video can last for several years without seeming dated, so long as it is produced with this in mind. This is partly a matter of following the rules on communication.

For example, if you refer to a news story that is in everyone's mind at the time when you make the video, you will need to explain it so that people who are watching in a few months' time, or next year, will still get the point. If you are discussing something financial, such as social security benefit rates or pay rates, you may need to put them in general terms or give the date that they relate to. You can then give specific details, or update the figures, in a background leaflet to be handed out at the same time.

Production

A few organisations now have their own production facilities, and people working for them with the right skills. If you are part of a larger campaign, or the branch of a union, check with your head office about the position.

Otherwise, there are video production houses. Some of them operate as companies on their own, while others are part of larger public relations firms. There are large numbers in London, and smaller numbers in other major cities. Go to one that will be generally sympathetic to your aims, which might mean a BECTU-franchised workshop. (BECTU is the union covering the industry, and it has special arrangements for a number of video-workshops which work closely with campaigning groups and trade unions). Ask BECTU nationally for details of workshops in your area (see Appendix 2: Addresses).

You will get the best results if you know exactly what you want, and are demanding about it. If instead you go with a vague idea that, 'we want something that tells people about this issue,' you will get the producer's idea of what the issue is, and what will be interesting to the public about it, rather than your own.

So before you start talking to anyone, write a rough draft of the sort of publicity leaflet that you would use to persuade people to take the video. Work out:

- who you want it to be seen by; and
- what you want to tell them.

Add a brief summary of what your organisation's aims are, and what it does (as explained on page 6). When talking to the producers, you will be dealing with people who know of you only vaguely, if at all.

Then ring or write to the various production houses, and find out if they are interested. Send them your draft, and make an appointment to visit them and meet the people who would work on it. Ask to be shown round, and to see the facilities available. Try also to see an example of something that they have already produced. Find out their ideas on how they would turn your draft into a programme, how long it would take, and how much it would cost. Discuss also who would hold the copyright, how many free copies you would get as part of the deal, and the price of extra copies.

Ask them to put down their ideas, and rough costings, in writing, and send them to you within a reasonable time. This is partly a test of whether they'll keep to time if you commission them to make the video. If they can't write a letter when they say they are going to, they probably can't meet a video deadline either.

Before finally deciding who to use, think about:

- Whether they are reasonably sympathetic to your ideas.
- Whether they have been able to communicate easily with you, explaining the technicalities in everyday terms.
- Whether you like them as people. You are going to work closely with them over quite a long time, so this is important.

Once you have committed yourselves, you will be asked to sign a *contract*, and to agree a *schedule*. Look at these carefully. Check the reasons that they can come back to you for more money, and the timetable they expect to work to. If it's unrealistic for you, get it adjusted at this stage. Once the schedule slips, it will be very difficult to catch up on the lost time.

On average, you should allow three or four months to get a good-quality video, commissioned by you as client, from the stage of a firm agreement to do it, to the final product. Out of this, a week or so will be spent filming. The rest of the time will go on consulting and agreeing on the script, research, deciding what to film and what goes on the soundtrack, and editing and finishing off the videotape.

The plan for what is being filmed and recorded is called the 'treatment' and will probably go through several drafts. The organisation commissioning the video ought to approve the treatment before shooting (filming) starts. Make sure this is included in the schedule. Decide who in your group has the power to give approval. Make sure that they have the time available at the right point. This person will need to be able to turn around the draft quickly when it comes to him or her, in order not to hold up the process.

If the early drafts of the treatment are not what you want, say so. Video-makers expect to develop their ideas by arguing them out. But remember that each rewriting will add a week or a fortnight to your timetable. There may come a point where you decide to let them go ahead, rather than fiddle around with the drafts any longer.

If things go badly wrong, it may be best to cut your losses and halt the whole process, rather than spending more money on something you will not dare show your members or supporters. Make sure you are satisfied with what you will be getting *before* filming starts. The cost of changing anything after that mounts up sharply.

Filming

This section is not intended to be a technical guide to the 'right' sort of shots to take. The people doing the production work should know the techniques and what will work well or badly. Here, we give only a few points to look out for:

- A mixture of different sorts of short graphics, interviews, 'action pictures', is best. People do not want to concentrate on anything for very long. You will be able to keep the cost down, for pictures of places or objects, if you use 'library film'. This is film that has already been taken for another purpose, re-used. Alternatively, standard shots – of an office block or a shop for instance, can be filmed close to the production base, to keep down the travel costs.

- Keep the graphics simple, even if your computer is clever at creating fancy ones. Each chart or graph should make just one point. If you want to use symbols in your charts – like the common one of piles of coins and notes when you are talking about money – make sure they are appropriate to what you want to illustrate, and easily understandable by your audience.

- If you are quoting someone, and want people to remember it, put the words on the screen while the voice is reading them. If quotes or figures are particularly important, you could also put them in the background material or handout.

- Aim for a mix of men and women, black and white, old and young people appearing. Try also to have a mix of different accents, rather than have everyone talking BBC English.

- If you can get a celebrity or 'big name' to appear free, it will usually be worth it. But if s/he has an image which is at odds with the message you are putting across, you may need to decline an offer gracefully. Be wary of offers to take part for 'expenses only'.

Get these clarified before you accept. Some people's expenses can come in pretty high!

- It is cheaper, and often easier, to bring the people appearing in the video to the camera crew, rather than sending the crew to them. You will probably need to do some location work, to illustrate your points adequately, but try to keep the number of different locations as low as possible.

It will usually be sensible for the person who is liaising with the production house to go along with them when they are filming. It's not essential, though, if you trust the producer. But you should ask to see the 'offline' (the tape before it is finally edited). If the quality of a particular section seems poor, or if you very much dislike something, say so now before the final edition. Re-shooting is always possible, though it will add to the cost.

Background material

It's common, and helpful, for videos to be distributed along with a background leaflet or information pack. For this, the same rules of good communication apply as for anything else. In addition:

- Think about how it will be used. If the video is mainly a teaching aid, and you expect it to be used with a tutor present, then prepare an extra, more detailed set of notes for the tutor. Suggest additional points s/he might like to cover, and tasks s/he might like the group to undertake – like investigating or debating a particular subject.

- Design the leaflet or briefing pack to look good, and to key in with the images in the video. If you can, find the money to print it in colour, with good quality pictures. Otherwise, keep it plain but try at least to print the cover in colour. Use the same logo on the leaflet or pack as on the video. It's a good idea for each copy of the video to have a printed card on it, to show what it is and who it comes from. Make sure it fits in also with the background pack.

- Link the discussion notes firmly back to the content of the video. For instance, you could use a comment by an interviewee, or an incident on the tape, as a starting point. You might also want to include an exercise for people to do before watching the video. This could then alert them to particular themes and issues and suggest that they watch out for them. This tends to focus people's attention, and can liven up discussion afterwards.

- Include a note of other things they might read, or other videos to see. Include a membership form too, or a note of where people can obtain information about your organisation. Even if it is to be seen mainly by supporters, other people are likely also to get hold of it or to attend meetings where it is being shown, and it would be good to stimulate their interest as well.

- Mention the fact that there is background material on the video itself, at the end with the credits. Some people are bound to see it at times and places where the background material is not available, so give an address to which they can write off for it.

Distribution

How can you make sure that people are going to see your videos? You need to decide on the method of distribution, the uses to which you want them put, and the audiences you hope for, before you ever start commissioning a video – for financial reasons if no other.

The three main possibilities are *loaning* tapes, *selling them*, or *giving* them away. Lending tapes out to your branches is relatively straight-forward, but lending them to total strangers may not be. It means keeping a stock, setting up arrangements to record who has what, and chasing up what does not come back.

The advantage of loans is that they are very cheap for the user, who only has to pay the cost of postage. They also give the group information about who is seeing the tape, and a chance to receive comments on it. Some at least of the borrowers will complete a questionnaire included in the pack to be sent back.

If you sell the tapes, the price may be too high for some people, and you are unlikely to get information back from those who buy. Some organisations may want to see the tape just once, and discuss the issues anyway, before moving on to something else. They could feel it was wasteful to buy a tape, and so be discouraged from looking at it at all.

Giving tapes away does not have these disadvantages – but it is expensive.

It is best – though it may not be practical for everyone – to mix the three methods. Keep a stock of tapes to lend out to close contacts like your own branches or groups similar to yours. Try to persuade other organisations that lend videotapes, like some public libraries, and some trade unions, to stock yours. Keep a list of those who do so, so you can refer people to them. You might also want to persuade organisations who do not at present run tape libraries to start doing so. For instance, if your tape is about a local issue and you know that there are others about problems in the area, you could suggest to the local Council for Voluntary Service or Trades Council that they start a tape library.

You can then sell tapes at a price that takes account of at least part of the production costs to anyone else, along with the background material.

Finally, you might want to give some tapes away free, perhaps to policy makers or groups of supporters with no money.

The sale or loan of non-commercial videos is done almost entirely by mail order. Telling people they exist and where to get them, involves getting information into the right places. You can do this by:

- Printing a small leaflet, and handing it out at meetings of the people you want to contact, or putting it in your mailings, or those of other people (see Chapter 11 for ideas on this).

- Putting advertisements in the newspapers and magazines that are read by the people you want to contact, or by using any free 'notice-board' facility that will reach the people you want.

- Sending free copies of the video to the magazines or journals to review, as you would a book, or sending out a news release and persuading them to cover it as news or a feature. See pages 179–84 for details of how to write and send news releases.

PART IV
The media

16

Working with the media

What are the media?

'Media' is the word used to cover newspapers, magazines, TV and radio as a whole. It is a Latin word, and means roughly, 'those in the middle.' Most of the time the media are between you and your target audience.

What appears in the media is written or spoken by someone else, and they are in control. But you can control the material you feed to them and the impression you give. The average reporter is rushed off his or her feet, and under stress. Most of them know very little about the subjects they write or talk about. If you hand over well-presented facts and figures on a plate, and do or say things that are going to come over well, you improve the chances that you will be well-reported – though you can never count on it.

Who should you be contacting?
Your first step is to work out which newspaper, magazine or programme is going to be most useful to you. Ask:

– who is my target audience (as explained in Chapter 2); and
– what will they read, or what programme will they follow?

Think about whether your target audience is *local* or *national*, and whether it is *specialist* in your subject, or *general*. Then build up a list of the media that fit the pattern.

Media to think about

This section looks at the printed media – newspapers and magazines. The next one covers TV and radio.

Newspapers and magazines can be divided into a number of groups:

National 'qualities' (sometimes also called 'broadsheets'). These appeal mainly to the middle classes, professional and business people. In February 1991, their average daily sales ranged between 400,000 each for *The Times*, *The Guardian* and *The Independent*, and 1.1m for *The Daily Telegraph*.

Circulations and influence do not match. In the City and among employers, for instance, the *Financial Times* with a readership of only 2 per cent of the total population is vastly more influential than *The Daily Telegraph* with five or six times the circulation.

'Tabloid' newspapers These have much larger circulations, and a much lower amount of news in each edition. Much of what there is, is gossip about royalty, the stars of soap operas, or footballers. They are written in very much simpler language than the qualities, with short words and sentences. Surveys show that the readers take much less notice of what they read in these papers than they do of the TV and radio reporters, and do not believe very much of it.

The highest selling tabloid newspaper is *The Sun*, with 26 per cent of the *total* market in February last year. The *Daily Mirror*, *Daily Express* and *Daily Mail* each sell in their millions, while the *Daily Star*, *Today* and the Scottish *Daily Record* sell hundreds of thousands.

On Sundays, the most popular paper is the *News of the World*, which sells 5m copies. The biggest selling quality is *The Sunday Times* with 1.2m, while the other qualities sell between 400,000 and 600,000.

The national newspapers are owned by a small number of people and organisations. For example, Rupert Murdoch, through his company News International, owns *The Times* and *The Sunday Times*, the *News of the World*, *Today*, and *The Sun*.

Regional daily papers Most major cities outside London have their own evening papers, and sometimes a morning paper as well. London has only the *Evening Standard*.

Many of these have a high percentage readership in their own areas, and are read by people from all social groups. *Far* more people will read the local paper in almost any area, than will read a national quality paper. The majority of local papers are owned by a few large groups, several of whom have other media interests as well.

Local weekly papers Almost every town has at least one local weekly paper. There are two kinds, the 'paid-fors' and the 'free newspapers' or 'freebies'. The paid-fors contain rather more news, and are probably read with more care than the freebies, but people do take notice of what is in these also. The freebies particularly tend to have very small reporting staffs, and are mainly vehicles for advertising.

To understand how regional and local newspapers work, two useful books are *News in the Regions*, by Alastair Hetherington, and *What News; the market, politics and the local press*, by Murphy and Franklin (see

Appendix 1: Booklist for details). They explain what they look for, and how they collect and analyse their stories.

'General' magazines These include the weekly equivalent of the 'quality' newspapers, such as the *New Statesman and Society*, *The Spectator*, and *The Economist*. They have small circulations but some influence among the policy-makers.

Then there are the women's magazines, which have very large circulations (well over a million, in some cases). There are the cheaper weekly ones, such as *Woman* and *Woman's Own*, and the expensive monthly ones like *Good Housekeeping* and *Cosmopolitan*. Among women, they are influential in forming opinions, and can often take quite radical approaches. They plan their coverage months in advance, and have very specific styles. If you want them to accept your material, you need to fit in with these.

Specialist magazines and newspapers There are hundreds of these, covering every sort of trade, profession and hobby. Most trade unions publish their own magazines for their members, and so do many membership organisations. There are also newspapers and magazines for ethnic minority groups, some of them written in their mother tongue, and for religious groups. They divide into those sold at newsagents, those that are sent through the post on subscription, and those that are 'controlled circulation.' This means that they are sent free to everyone who belongs to a certain profession, or has reached a particular level in a business. On many subjects, there is one leading magazine that forms opinions and is read by everyone, and the rest are followers.

Many magazines are owned by large companies – in some cases the same people as own national and local newspapers.

Who reads what?

A good local paper will have a big circulation in the immediate area, and will be read in depth by people across all social groups. Local papers are studied quite closely, especially the letters page – and what is said is remembered.

Scotland and Northern Ireland's papers are national rather than regional; far more people will buy them as their *only* papers than in England. The *Daily Record*'s 800,000 circulation in Scotland for instance, gives it much closer to saturation coverage there than *The Sun*'s 3.7m gives it for the UK as a whole. The *Scotsman* and the *Glasgow Herald* sell about 90,000 and 125,000 respectively, while *The Guardian* and *The Independent* sell only about 16,000 each in Scotland.

The national qualities have to spread half a million copies or so across the whole population. So in the average town, there may be no more than a hundred copies sold. Several of them will probably go to people who are already involved in your group, or with their minds made up about your cause. So a story in one of these papers could be preaching to the local converted.

On the other hand, it might influence policy-makers in Whitehall or Westminster, or spread the message about what you are doing elsewhere.

Local politicians and council officials will read national newspapers, but will also look carefully at the local papers. *National* politicians in Whitehall and Westminster will take little notice of local papers, but will pay attention to what is in both the qualities and the tabloids.

A group that wants to deal mainly with professionals – perhaps to influence the way doctors deal with a particular group of patients, for example – will want to contact the specialist magazines, and the papers those professionals are likely to read.

Checking the list

Having drawn up a draft list of the newspapers and magazines you are interested in, check it with a few other sources.

Local Councils of Voluntary Service in some areas publish directories of local media. If your local CVS does not provide a directory, ask them to start doing so.

Your public library probably has most of the national daily papers, and the local papers, though they may not stock all the free advertising sheets.

A big central reference library, or a library in a university or college, may have the main specialist magazines as well.

To find out about local newspapers and specialist magazines, the best guide is BRAD (British Rates and Advertising Digest). This is updated each month, and lists all the papers and magazines published in the UK. It is expensive to subscribe to, but if you have a contact involved with advertising or the media, he or she may be willing to pass on last month's copy when the new one comes out. That would be up-to-date enough for most purposes.

There are also other directories such as Willings, Benn's and PIMS, which are updated less regularly, but which may be in the main reference library near you. Figure 16.1 is an example of a typical entry from Benn's, to give you an idea of what is included.

Find out the names of the editors, their news and features editors, and the reporters most likely to be covering any story about your group and the issues you are dealing with. PIMS will give much of this information, but look at the papers or magazines themselves as well. Most of them list their editors and perhaps other reporters somewhere, perhaps on the middle 'editorial' page for newspapers, or the contents

Figure 16.1

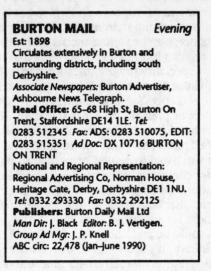

```
BURTON MAIL                Evening
Est: 1898
Circulates extensively in Burton and
surrounding districts, including south
Derbyshire.
Associate Newspapers: Burton Advertiser,
Ashbourne News Telegraph.
Head Office: 65–68 High St, Burton On
Trent, Staffordshire DE14 1LE. Tel:
0283 512345 Fax: ADS: 0283 510075, EDIT:
0283 515351 Ad Doc: DX 10716 BURTON
ON TRENT
National and Regional Representation:
Regional Advertising Co, Norman House,
Heritage Gate, Derby, Derbyshire DE1 1NU.
Tel: 0332 293330 Fax: 0332 292125
Publishers: Burton Daily Mail Ltd
Man Dir: J. Black Editor: B. J. Vertigen.
Group Ad Mgr: J. P. Knell
ABC circ: 22,478 (Jan–June 1990)
```

page for magazines. Look at the names on the different articles, to see who writes what sort of piece. (A few magazines don't give the names of their writers.) If you want to know more about who does what, phone and ask the person on the switchboard, or the editor's secretary.

The editorial page, and BRAD, will give a figure for circulation, but it won't be broken down into geographical areas or professions. For extra information on this, phone up the advertising department. There would be no harm in implying that you were thinking of advertising in that magazine. If you want to find out how many of a particular national or regional paper are read in your area, try asking a few local newsagents how many copies are regularly ordered, and multiply this upwards to get a rough figure.

Try to get a 'feel' for each publication. Someone from your group should read it regularly, or at least occasionally, and chat to others who do so also, to find out what they think about it. You could spread this task out among different members of the group.

TV and radio

TV and radio programmes do not divide in quite the same way as newspapers and magazines. Broadly speaking, there are the news programmes, which are watched or listened to by a wide cross section of the population; the current affairs programmes like *Panorama* and

Newsnight, watched by much smaller audiences, often those with some political concern; and the more popular programmes like the Jimmy Young show and similar ones on local radio. *Woman's Hour* on Radio 4 covers a wider group than many other programmes and can have a wide influence, but the various special women's magazines that have been tried on television have not succeeded in the same way.

There are also specialist programmes for particular groups, like people with disabilities, farmers, people belonging to ethnic minorities.

Figures for the audiences for programmes can be obtained from the information officer or press officer for that station. For local TV and radio, the important figure is the 'reach' – what proportion of the *potential* audience listens. This varies considerably. Half the population in the local area will listen to Radio Cornwall at some time in a week – while Radio Manchester only reaches 16 per cent in a week.

Two organisations called JICTAR and JICRAR commission surveys these figures, and distribute them to the TV and radio companies. Summaries of them are published each month in a magazine called *Broadcast*. This should be available in a business library or possibly a main reference library. It's possible, but extremely expensive, to buy a set of the detailed ratings for each programme, but it's not likely that you'd ever need to. The press or public relations officer of the TV or radio station may well be willing to give you the information about a particular programme, if you have a good reason for asking.

Find out the same information about TV and radio programmes in your locality, or of special interest to your group, as for the newspapers or magazines. Ask for volunteers to watch or listen to them regularly, if not every time.

News in the Regions, referred to above, covers the news programmes in its chosen areas in detail, and will give you some idea of the approach used. There is also a book called *Get it On*, (see Appendix 1: Booklist for details) which is rather London-oriented, and also out of date now, but includes a directory of programmes and their various approaches. It is still worth using as a starting point.

The Press Association

The Press Association (PA) should be on everyone's contact list. It is a national news service that goes out to all newspapers, TV and radio programmes, both local and national. You can send it news releases, or phone up with a story, in just the way you would for any other part of the media. Its reporters then write up the story, usually fairly briefly, and send it out 'over the wires', by fax machine, or directly into the computer systems of newspapers, radio and TV stations. The journalists putting together a paper or a programme will check what has come in from the PA. They may well use a PA story with very little rewriting, or they may follow it up in more detail themselves.

Using your list

Use your contact list selectively. Send out a press release or an invitation to those for whom it is suitable, rather than to everyone on the list. Even with a group that's doing work of national importance, some of your stories are only going to be interesting to local people in the area around the project, or to specialists. For example:

Anytown Alzheimer's Disease Group wants people in the town to know what it is doing, so all the local newspapers, TV and radio are on its list. It's also doing some unusual work that people having to cope with Alzheimer's Disease (senile dementia), might like to know about. So the specialist magazines dealing with social work, and the care of elderly people, are also on the list. They get the news releases about that work, but not about the coffee mornings and jumble sales.

Divide up your contact list into different categories, and decide which category each news release is going to. Then draft it with that fact in mind.

Those not on your 'useful' list

Keep an eye on the papers and programmes that you have left off your list because they are not read by the right people, as well as those that are. They might carry a story that could damage you, or have information that could be useful. If one of them seems to be showing a lot of interest in the subject, or to have changed their attitude, add them to your list. It needs reviewing at least once a year in any case.

You may be able to 'recycle' publicity you get in media who are not on your list. You could, for instance, reprint an article as part of a leaflet (with their permission) or issue a news release about the fact that it is appearing, or tell your supporters about it in advance and encourage them to buy copies.

With TV, people will put themselves out to watch a programme on a subject they are interested in or about something local, even if it is on a channel and at a time when they would not normally watch. So it is worth using your best public relations efforts to make sure that those you are trying to influence know about it. You could, for instance, try to get your local paper to run a feature about the making of the programme, or arrange for a transcript of an interview to be reprinted in one of the magazines covering the subject.

A good rule of thumb for publications and programmes not on your list is to be helpful if they contact you, but not to make efforts to call them. This is true even when you feel the outfit is likely to be hostile. You are likely to get an even worse press out of refusing to comment, than if you do attempt to put your side of the story.

Going outside your list

There will also be occasions when you want to go outside your normal list for special reasons. Examples might be:

- Where you are taking up a case from, or running an event in, a particular part of the country. Send your news releases then to the main newspapers and programmes in that area.

- Where there's an audience that would not usually be interested in the points you want to make, but you have a story that will be of concern to them. A trade union, for instance, might want to send details about a dispute to a trade journal or a pressure group's magazine, if it was likely to affect their readers.

- When someone from a different walk of life says or does something in your 'patch'. For instance, a leading cleric might say something about your topic; you could then send your news release to the *Church Times, The Tablet,* or another religious paper, depending on their denomination.

To find out who to contact, look in BRAD or PIMS (explained on page 166) or go into the nearest reference library and look at the magazines on display. Or phone up any contacts you have and ask their advice. When you have the names of some publications, phone their switchboard and ask for the names of the right people to make contact with. Or simply send the news release to the editor, who will pass it on to whoever he or she thinks best.

For local papers in an area you don't know, PA (see page 168) may be interested if it is something they consider really important. Finding out about the local papers in the area will be more work, but more likely to produce results. If you've got no time or resources for anything else, look in the Yellow Pages for the area, which will probably be in your local library.

Major stories

If you have a major story, but very little time, then contact first of all the paper that you most want it to appear in. Then (unless you want it to be an 'exclusive') get through to the Press Association. See Appendix 2: Addresses for their address and phone number.

Monitoring media coverage

Someone – either the Media Officer or another person on the committee – should have the job of monitoring the coverage that's given to your group, and to the issues that the group is interested in. See the next chapter for ideas about how to do this, and what to look out for.

17

Dealing with media people

What are they interested in?

The media are in business to survive and, if possible, to make a profit. To do that, they must sell enough copies of their newspapers or magazines, and receive a steady flow of advertising.

Each part of the media aims to cater for different segments of the public. Therefore, they concentrate on issues that they believe will be important to them, while not bothering with others. They tend not to do detailed market research to find out about this. Instead the journalists base their ideas on what they or their friends think, or what people in the pub say.

So *The Guardian*, for instance, considers its readers are interested in civil liberties and will run stories about telephone tapping. *The Daily Telegraph* would be less likely to.

Certain newspapers have obsessions about certain subjects, and will print, and follow up over a long period of time, almost any story that will fit in with them. In London, for instance, the *Evening Standard* tends to print stories that illustrate its idea of 'Loony Left' Labour councils. It's often accused of ignoring stories about sensible things they are doing, though its editor would deny this.

There's also a tendency within the media to have a 'flavour of the month'. That is, they concentrate on a particular issue for a short time, and then lose interest and switch to something else. This is partly because they are afraid that the readers or audience will get bored; it's perhaps rather more that the journalists themselves get bored quickly. For example in 1990, the environment and Europe seemed to be flavours of the month – at least until the situation in the Gulf began taking over more and more pages.

Finally, there's a certain element of chance about which stories get into newspapers and which do not. Some days are much busier than others, and if an important event happens, it will take up a lot of space. The story that might otherwise have been printed that day will be lost. It probably won't be used the next day, because it will be considered 'dead news'. The effects of a really major story will run for several days and squeeze out a great deal else. The attempted coup against Gorbachev in the Soviet Union in August 1991, for instance, took over a large amount of space in papers that would otherwise have been scratching around for news during the 'silly season'.

If this happens to a story in which you have spent time and effort, you have to regard it as just bad luck. There is not a lot you can do about it at the time. But you may be able to think of a way of repackaging the story later on, highlighting a different point, and sending out a further set of news releases about it.

Newsworthiness

This is the word used by editors and reporters about any topics they want to cover. They often do not define it very closely, but they'll have (or believe they have) a 'feel' for what their readers or audience wants. It will be different for each publication or programme, but there will be common points. Every story needs to:

– have a definite point to it, which can be got over quickly;
– be happening now, or very soon, or have happened recently, so that it is topical;
– involve human beings (or animals), preferably ones who can be named and make brief comments – and for many publications also provide good photographs.

The specialist publications will not worry so much about 'human interest'. But they do want information that is new, that builds on or contradicts earlier stories they have printed, and that stands up to examination by other specialists. Anything claiming to be research, for instance, has to show that it is based on facts rather than guesswork, and needs to be able to quote sources for what is being said.

Making yourselves newsworthy

Making sure that you offer the right stories to the right place mainly means following the rules of good communication outlined in Chapter 3. For this purpose, the media, and not the general public, are your target audience. So start from what their position is. Take into account what they know and don't know, and what will attract them.

The fact that you raised £99 at your jumble sale will be interesting for the paper read by the people in the local area, who might have come along. So it is newsworthy for that paper, but for the regional TV programme it won't be. But they might be interested if you have a celebrity opening it, or if someone found a wallet full of money in the pocket of an old jacket. Having caught their interest, then it's up to you to make sure they know what your organisation is and what it does.

You may be able to turn a story that is not newsworthy into one that is, without changing its message, by creating an 'angle'. Is there a gimmick you can use to get your point across, or a big name you can enrol? Is there a person who would allow you to use their story to illustrate the point you want to make? Can you get a local MP to make a speech about the issue in the House of Commons, or to attend your meeting? Is there some research you can do, that will demonstrate it?

Here are some examples of the way groups have made their message newsworthy:

- Save Child Benefit got some celebrities to present a giant shopping list to 10 Downing Street, with all the items that could have been bought with Child Benefit if it had been uprated.

- An advice agency used the example of a homeless woman and her children, who had been given a Social Fund loan to buy a tent, to demonstrate the problems being caused by the Fund.

- Kids' Club Network contacted all the education authorities in the country to find out how many had taken up the government's plea to set up after school clubs for children. They found that very few had done so, and issued a report to say so.

Whatever the story, write your news releases as plainly and simply as you can. Don't try to imitate journalists' language or be 'clever'. That's their job.

Using individuals' stories

Never use an individual's name without their permission. If you want to use the case but to protect their identity, don't describe too closely the part of the town they live in, and change the names, and perhaps also the sex and ages of the children. But say you are doing this, so that you can't be accused of inaccuracy. The standard sentence that is used in these cases is:

> The stories in this report are true, but the names and some of the personal details have been altered to protect the individuals.

The media, particularly TV and radio, may contact you to ask for more details, and to try to interview the people whose story you have used. Giving an interview is likely to help the chances of the story being used. Check with the people concerned before you ever give the story to the press, whether they are willing. You can then include it in the news release or elsewhere.

It's *very* important to make sure that people understand what is involved. Being filmed or interviewed can be nerve-racking, and the media can be insensitive when a person is distressed or under pressure. If the story is controversial, the person may find they receive hate-mail or hostile comments from their neighbours.

Don't pander to them

You do *not* have to write news releases for the tabloids that cater for the bottom end of the market, about nineteen-year-old bimbos and toyboys, simply because that is the way their reporters write their articles. It's very unlikely that *The Sun* would need to figure on your contact list, because they won't consider their readers are interested in your type of campaign. So they wouldn't use your news release, however hard you work at putting it in their style.

They are probably right, at least while those readers are spending their ten minutes looking at *The Sun* or similar papers. People read them for sex, sport, and a laugh, and they don't particularly want to be bothered with other things while doing so. But the same people might well be interested in your campaign when they read about it in the local paper, or a women's magazine, or see it on the regional TV news programme when they are more in the mood.

You don't need to ask for trouble either, though. Journalists on the tabloids read other newspapers, and pick up stories that seem to fit in with their own brand of news. Without distorting things or moving away from your objectives, you can do your best not to give them the chance. If you are planning something that could be labelled 'Loony Left' for instance, think first:

- What arguments would I use to convince the ordinary person in the street that what I am doing is correct and sensible?
- If I can't convince the person in the street, or am not given the chance to do so, will mud-slinging do more harm to the project's overall objectives than the good that particular activity would do?

You may want to go ahead anyway. But you may also find that there are some details you can alter, or some points you can give more prominence to, that would not harm your objectives.

Working with journalists

It's best to have just one person to coordinate contacts with the media, to send out news releases and deal with enquiries.

Journalists find it easiest to deal with one main person in a group, preferably with someone else acting as back-up if the first person is away. They are busy people, and want to be able to telephone quickly, both during the day and in the evenings. They will usually have a deadline to meet, and so they must be able to find someone who knows how to deal with them and answer their questions. They do *not* want to be transferred from one extension to another, or told to phone someone else's home number, or to overhear whispered conversations at the other end of the line saying, 'Does anyone know what our policy on X is?'

Possible ways of dealing with this are:

- Give the task of dealing with the media to someone who's already got a role, like the secretary, the convenor, or the paid director of the organisation. This often works well, but they may be too busy to do the job properly. Channelling all the information through the person who already has a lot of power in the organisation could also make others feel left out.

- Appoint a media officer, who does not have another role within the organisation, then channel all contacts with the media through him or her. This is probably the better method, and in the rest of this section it's assumed that this is what's happening. The person doing the work with the media is going to be referred to as the media officer, although in your organisation they may have a different job or title.

Whichever method you choose, work other than direct contact with the media can still be spread out within the organisation. Monitoring news coverage, for example, can be allocated to someone else. News releases can be sent out by the media officer, but drafted by and including quotes from the person actually working on the issue. When journalists phone with a query, the media officer can be the one who answers in the first instance. If they want to talk in depth the journalist can be passed on to the person really working on the subject.

It's also possible to rotate the work of dealing with the media, with different members of the organisation taking it on over a period of time. But do this over a fairly long time-scale – at least six months or a year. Or have annual elections for the job, or an annual share-out of the work.

Whoever is doing this job *must* have access to a phone, for incoming and outgoing calls, both at home and at work. The group should arrange to pay for the phone calls.

It is important – especially if the job is going to change hands – to have things written down, with a proper contacts file and files of past news releases and media coverage. They must be kept in a form which anyone can understand, and fully up to date. It could also be useful to have a small library of the main books about working with the media (see Appendix 1: Booklist) and details of where further information can be found.

Other people in the organisation should know where the contacts file is, and be entitled to look at it. Even if the job is not going to change hands often, the media officer could fall ill, or go on holiday. An open file also reduces the chances of a media officer building a little empire – deliberately or accidentally – where only they know what to do and who to contact.

It's a two-way process. The media officer needs the full cooperation of the rest of the organisation, and needs to know what is going on. A query may come up at any time on the work you are doing, which the media officer has to deal with. Or something may be planned which has scope for publicity work, if it is run in a particular way. So the media officer needs to know about it in enough time to influence the planning. People who are dealing with the media tend to develop a 'nose' for the good news angle, and can often see very quickly how to turn an unpromising story into a newsworthy one.

The media officer also needs to know about mistakes and possible disasters. The earlier s/he is aware of something coming up that may damage the organisation, the better s/he can plan how to respond. For example:

> One of the workers in the Hillside Housing Association is facing a lot of hostility from a group of tenants. A senior worker is trying to help calm the situation down. They have not yet told the management committee or the staff meeting about the problems. But they mention the difficulties to the media officer, in confidence, so that if one of the tenants goes to the newspapers s/he will be prepared and able to reply.

Making informal contact

One of the media officer's jobs is to keep in informal contact with journalists, so that they know who to get in touch with, and how to find out information when they need it. As suggested on page 163, the first task is to create the list of useful publications and programmes, and find the names of the key reporters on these. Then the media officer should gradually make contact with each of them, and continue afterwards to phone up anyone new who appears on the scene. S/he needs to:

– introduce him/herself and the organisation;
– ask whether the person needs any background information; and
– offer a general invitation to come in for a chat sometime.

The invitation is unlikely to be taken up, since most reporters are too busy, but it will break the ice.

Beyond that, a group that has the resources and is taking a high profile within the media could work positively at establishing that they are *the* source of information to come to, on that particular subject. This is how many national groups, ranging from Greenpeace to the BMA, managed to get publicity. They issue a steady stream of news releases with solid facts and stories in them. They also cultivate the media – inviting them to lunch or a drink, supplying background material whenever requested, and telling the journalists where to go for other material, and reacting quickly when something important happens.

Journalists will often use the facts that you have supplied without saying where they have come from. This may be irritating, but it is in fact a help to your cause. It will appear that the point you are making is 'received wisdom', rather than just an opinion of yours.

It's essential that any background information is correct, and you must have the facts at your fingertips, which could mean doing a lot of research. You must also put the points over in a reasonably objective way – including telling the reporter what the opposite point of view would be. Some organisations, like the British Medical Association, keep a list of possible speakers on a subject, including details of people who *disagree* with their point of view. This means that the reporters can get together a balanced story putting both sides of the argument.

Taking up your campaign

Many local newspapers – some more than others – make a habit of running campaigns on particular issues, or adopt causes for fund-raising activities over a long period of time.

The issues will usually be straightforward, easy to explain, and the sort to catch the imagination of the readers. Often, they will have something to do with children, or cancer, or a dangerous road or site.

If your organisation or campaign falls into the right category, it could be worth suggesting to the editor of a local newspaper that they adopt you as a cause, and run a series of stories over a period of time. This would give you a guarantee of wide publicity, but on the other hand you might have to adapt your activities, and possibly also your message, to fit in with the editor's news values. Think hard about whether you could do this without having to move away for your objectives. Look in your local paper for examples of their recent campaigns, to help yourself judge.

If you decide that it is worth doing, try to make contact with the editor directly. Go along with a prepared note about why the paper should adopt you, and some ideas about activities that could be featured. But be ready to show that you can adapt to the editor's own ideas. Don't let yourself come across as too dogmatic.

If you get agreement in principle, you'll then need to work closely with the newspaper over a period of time. Find out what their requirements are on deadlines, photographs, access to material and so on, and stick closely to them. Ask the editor to appoint one member of staff (perhaps him/herself) with whom you can liaise. Your group should appoint someone as a contact as well.

Being adopted is likely to mean that the newspaper wants exclusive coverage of your events, or at least the first bite of the cherry. Check this out with them, and keep to the agreement, even if other reporters try to persuade you to do something different. The agreement for TV and radio may be different from those for rival newspapers. The editor may be happy to let you have coverage, especially if the paper's name can be worked into the story.

The more carefully you plan and establish ground rules from the start, the more likely it is that the relationship will be a success.

Sending out news releases

Who to send these to was covered on page 169.

News releases are the raw material for most journalists most of the time. They are short typed statements – one, or at most two pages long. They give the story and tells the reporters who to contact for more information.

There's a particular method of writing news releases, and it is important to follow it wherever you can. Learning it is not difficult, and the method is there because it makes it easier for the reporter to select and shape the raw material s/he needs.

As each release comes into the office, someone glances quickly at it, throws it in the wastepaper basket if it is of no interest, or allocates it to be followed up if there seems to be an interesting story in it. The person doing the selection could be the editor, or a special member of staff doing just that job, or the reporter who covers a particular topic. So you have first to attract that person, and then you have to make it easy for the reporter to use your story.

The shorter and better written your release, the clearer your story, and the less work the reporter has to do on it, the greater the chances of its being used. In many local papers and magazines, news releases are used almost word for word in the smaller stories.

How to write a news release
There are two examples of news releases on pages 184–6. As you go through this section, look at them every so often and see how they match up with the guidelines given here.

Draft the news release roughly first – if necessary, several times. Even if you are pushed for time, write or type it out once at least, in full, before doing a final version.

The heading and first paragraph

These tell the reporter the story, fast. Your heading should be brief and plain, and sum up the point of the release. Don't try to write a headline – that's the reporter's job.

The first paragraph of the release is by far the most important. Spend as much time as you need on this. The basic facts, and the news angle, have to be in there, in whatever order reads best. It is this paragraph that will convince the reporter to keep your news releases on the desk, not in the wastepaper basket.

Try to include the 'five Ws', as they are called in reporters' jargon:

- Who?
- What?
- Where?
- When?
- Why?

although it is not always necessary to have each one in the first paragraph.

The rest of the news release

You now have a few hundred words in which to explain the details. This is your chance to get over your point of view, and the arguments you want to put. You need to keep the reporter's interest and, if possible, his/her sympathy. So:

- Keep it simple.
- Assume that the reporter knows absolutely nothing about the background.
- Make it human: give examples of people affected, and quotations from the people concerned, written in ordinary speech.

Say why things are happening. You might say, for instance, 'The County Council want to close the school because the number of pupils is falling.' Then say what the people involved feel, and the reasons that you believe you are right, and the others wrong.

Show that you are the reasonable ones, and your opponents are not. Give their arguments, in a factual way, and then explain why you don't agree. Don't use irony or sarcasm, as the uninformed reader may miss the point. Don't exaggerate or distort the other side's arguments.

You'd be caught out if the reporter then approaches them, as s/he is likely to.

If you're complaining about something, make clear what you are going to do about it.

Finish on an optimistic note – that you are going to win the industrial dispute, or raise so much money.

Putting in the important details

The reporter reading your news release needs to know more than just the news story. S/he also needs to know:

- Who is the group sending out the news release.
- Whether it is true, and how it can be checked.
- Extra details to fill out the report, if it is going to be longer than the original news release.

So the release has to be on *headed paper*, making plain who the organisation is, and where they are based. Many groups have special paper with 'News Release' printed in large letters at the top, beside the address and phone number. This looks impressive, but it is not necessary. If you are using ordinary headed paper, type NEWS RELEASE in capitals at the top. Put the date here, and again at the end of the news release.

Put on a Note to Editors at the end of the main release, explaining who your group is, and what your aims are. Use this Note to give any extra background information, or to say that photographers would be welcome, or that people will be available for interview.

Every news release must have a *name* at the bottom, or more than one. Usually this would be the media officer, or the person who is acting as a media contact for this purpose. There should also be contact numbers, preferably more than one. These need to be the work and home phone numbers of the people who are able to answer questions and give further information about the story. They could be the media officer, and the group's Chair or secretary, and another person to act as back-up. If people will have to move from work to home at some point, include the times when this will happen.

It is important to include work as well as home numbers. The reporters may well be putting the story together during the day, so that it goes to the printer in mid-afternoon or early evening. If they can't reach anyone in time, it will become out of date and not be used. If no one in the group is normally available on the phone during the day, someone might be able to make an arrangement with the employer, or the union office, to take calls and bring you to the telephone. If you had a major story and were keen to get media coverage, it could be necessary for someone to take the day off and stay by the phone at home.

With a topical story like the strike ballot in the example on page 185, the media contacts named in the news release might be phoned almost as soon as the release reached the office, and further questions asked. So they *must* be at the numbers given on the sheet when the release goes out.

How to deal with the media when they make contact is dealt with in Chapter 18.

The layout

The examples on pages 184–6 show how a news release is set out on the page. Type it, double spaced, with margins at least two inches wide so that the reporters can alter things or add in extra words when preparing it for the media. Keep the paragraphs short. Don't break up words with a hyphen at the end of a line. Carry them over to the next line instead. Try not to continue a paragraph on a second page – leave more space at the bottom of the page instead.

If your release takes up more than one page, number each one and put 'more' at the bottom left hand corner of each page except the last. Put 'ends' after the last line on the final page.

In the top right hand corner of each page except the first, put a 'strap line', which is a word or two words that will identify the story the news release is about, in case the different pages get separated. In the examples on pages 184–6, the strap lines might be 'Elmbank petition' for the first and 'Durlin ballot' on the second. Staple the pages together.

Photocopy your news release on a good machine, or print it out several times from a computer. Don't use carbons if you can avoid it. The people who get the carbon copies will feel that they are second-class citizens.

Deadlines, timing and embargoes

Any publication or programme has a deadline – that is, a time after which information that has come in can't be used because the newspaper or magazine is being typeset or the programme is being recorded. You can find out the deadline by phoning up and asking the editor, the editor's secretary, or one of the reporters. Typical deadlines would be:

- For a daily newspaper, somewhere between 3pm and 5pm the day before.
- For an evening newspaper, the previous afternoon for most stories, except for very major ones which could come in later.
- For a weekly paper, two days before the publication date, so Wednesday for a Friday publication.
- For a glossy weekly magazine, six weeks before publication.

- For a glossy monthly magazine, anything up to three months ahead.

There are exceptions to all these; weekly news magazines like *The Economist*, for instance, have the same deadlines as for weekly newspapers. The Saturday and Sunday papers' non-news sections, on the other hand, may be printed, or at least typeset, by the middle of the week. And while the weekly and monthly women's magazines have very long deadlines, because so many copies are printed, some of the small professional and 'trade' magazines, though just as glossy, are only printing a few thousand copies and can therefore have much later deadlines.

TV and radio programmes follow roughly the same pattern. For daily news programmes, the deadline will be very close to the time when the programme goes out; for weekly and monthly programmes which need research and recording, it will be much longer.

However, only important stories will actually be used if they turn up just before the deadline. Most campaigning groups' stories are not in that league, so try to get your material in as early in the day or the week, as you can.

This will often mean telling the media about something before it has actually happened. You might do this if you are sending a letter to a politician, or making an announcement about something, or holding an event. Send the news release several days before the official date. With the small staff many papers have these days, there are problems about using last minute news, because people will have already have been allocated to different stories.

Put on the news release, 'Not for publication before 00.01 hours on [the day it is actually happening].' This means the journalists should not use the story until the beginning of that day.

This is called an *embargo*, and reporters will usually respect it. They will break it, though, if you do so by 'going public' in advance of that date, or if one of their rivals does so, or they get wind that s/he is going to. Twenty-four hour embargoes are very common, and normally work successfully. Longer ones tend to break down.

If your event is taking place after the deadline, but before it is published, sending an advance news release is the only way in which you are likely to get publicity. By the time the next edition comes out, it will be 'dead news' as far as the media are concerned.

If the event is completely spontaneous or unpredictable, (or if you are trying to make people believe that it is), you won't be able to send an advance news release. But most of the events with which you will be involved will be planned in advance, and you know at least what *you* are going to do, even if you cannot tell how the other side will respond. So that gives you a chance to get your side of the story in first, so that the other side can only react.

Sometimes, you know that something important is going to be announced, but you won't know exactly what it is until the last minute. This could be the publication of a government report, or the announcement of a ballot result. You could prepare *two* news releases, to cover both options, in advance. Keep them in draft until you know what the result is, and only finalise the right one then. Re-read it carefully before sending it out, just in case something unexpected has happened and makes it look silly.

If you're sending out a news release after the event, then speed is vital. Twenty-four hours is normally the most you would be able to allow. Past events are dead news, as far as the media are concerned, and the 'past' is anything that happened before the previous edition was published. So for an evening newspaper or an evening news programme, only events that have happened that day are 'news'. For a morning paper or programme, events the day before are still topical – for a weekly, events the week before. But small weekly papers and specialist magazines for particular interest groups do often print material which is well out of date by anyone else's standards.

Two examples

Here are two examples of news releases, one issued before the event and one after:

Before the event

Heading	ELMBANK PETITION ABOUT DANGEROUS ROAD
Opening paragraph	
(who)	Elmbank School Action Group
(what)	will be presenting a petition
(where)	to the Council meeting at the Town Hall
(when)	on 23 March
(why)	to ask the Council to take action about the dangerous junction near the school
Explanation	Elmbank school is a large primary school on the West side of Anytown. It faces directly on to the busy Elmbank Road. Parents and teachers have been campaigning for action to make the road safer ever since a 10 year old boy was knocked down by a car in January. He was the fifth child to be hurt there in the last three years.

Quote 1	'Cars come round the corner at 40 or 50 miles an hour, and there is no sign warning of a school ahead,' said Mrs Jennifer Miles, one of the parents at the school. 'It's very lucky that no-one's been killed yet.'
More explanation	The group want a sign before the bend, and an island in the middle of the road. So far, they have written letters to their councillors and met the Chair of the Highways Committee, but there has been no action. They have now collected 500 signatures from local people in the streets around the school. Elmbank Ward Councillor Maden will be presenting their petition to the Mayor at the beginning of the meeting.
Quote 2	'The Councillors keep making sympathetic noises, but they don't do anything,' said Bill Henty, Secretary of the Action Group. 'We want them to realise how strongly people feel about
Ends	the issue, and take some action.'

Contact names and phone numbers
Date

Note to Editors	Elmbank School Action Group is a group of concerned parents and local residents at the school.
	The petition is being presented to Councillor Maden outside the Town Hall at 5.30 pm, by 20 members of the group, with banners. They will then go into the public gallery to watch him present the petition to the Mayor at 6.30. Reporters and photographers welcome. Bill Henty and Jennifer Miles will be available for interview before or after the event.

Immediately after the event

Heading	DURLIN WORKERS VOTE FOR STRIKE
Opening paragraph	
(who)	The 200 workers

(where)	at the Durlin Group factory in Eye Lane
(what)	today voted for strike action
(when)	to start next week
(why)	after management refused to concede a reduction in working hours.
Explanation	The vote came after the shop stewards had been attempting for over two months to negotiate the cut in working hours, without success. Proposals for the strike were put to the workforce in a secret ballot, and in a 75 per cent turnout they voted 3 to 1 in favour of the action.
	An indefinite strike is planned for Monday 23 March. The union has already set up a strike committee and arranged a picketing rota.
Quote 1	'It's the first time for over 20 years we have had to take a step like this,' said Pete Skerrow, union convenor. 'Management do not seem to understand how strongly the workers feel on this issue.'
More explanation	The union have proposed ways to cut the working week to 37 hours in two stages, and to shorten tea-breaks and washing up time. But this has been rejected by management, who have offered only half an hour off in return for major concessions on flexibility. The plant is owned by a West German company, and makes components for the auto industry.
Quote 2	'The workers at the plant have bent over backwards to accommodate management fears about productivity,' says union district official Tom Hood. 'I hope that now the employers realise that the workforce are serious about taking action, they will concede these very reasonable demands.'

Ends
Contact names and phone numbers
Date

Distribution

For a straightforward news release about something that is coming up in the future, or is not particularly urgent, use the first class post. For anything urgent, use a fax machine if you can afford it. They are now widely available in print shops and office service bureaux, and now occasionally in some resource centres, union offices and voluntary organisations. There has to be a fax machine at the other end also, to receive the message, but almost every media organisation has at least one today. Phone and ask for their fax number, if it is not on their notepaper.

Sending a fax is by far the best way to communicate an urgent message to the media. It is better than a telephone call, where the words may be misheard or noted down wrongly. However, faxes are expensive. Typically, sending a sheet of paper will cost £1 or so in a commercial firm, 70p in a non-profit making organisation.

Don't try to use a fax without permission. Most machines produce print-outs of the numbers that have been contacted, and the number from which a fax is sent often appears at the top of the page at the other end.

For something that's important just to one particular publication, you can telephone with a prepared statement. The reporter is likely to ask you further questions, so you need to have your replies ready.

Other ways of using news releases

There are several other ways in which news releases can be used:

- To give advance notice of an event that's coming up.
- To tell people what is going to be said, or has been said, in a speech.
- To draw the media's attention to a publication somewhere else, and give them details of what it says.

Giving advance notice

One of the key planning tools in the media is the diary of events that are coming up, or stories that they may want to cover at the right time. If something major comes up on that day, then the diary and the forward planning will be scrapped or very much altered. But in an ordinary week, many of the items you see in the media will have come out of the diary.

So, if you are planning something in the future that you think may interest the media, send out an advance notice. Three or four weeks ahead is reasonable, or longer if it is a major event and you want to negotiate special coverage. If the event is being set up at shorter notice, send the advance notice as soon as you can.

Send your news release to the journalist you want to cover the event, and also to the editor or producer. This should ensure that, even if the relevant person is on holiday or out covering another story, the item gets entered in the diary for future reference.

A few days before the event, phone up and check that the notice was received. Ask if someone will be attending. You are unlikely to get a definite answer, but it will jog memories and perhaps make them consider your event in their forward planning.

If royalty, a major politician or controversial figure is coming to your event, the police may ask you *not* to give publicity to the event until very shortly before it, for security reasons. You should still be able to send out an advance notice to the editors who need to know about it, making it clear that publicity is not wanted at this stage through an embargo (explained on page 183). Check with the police, or with the office of the person concerned, before doing so.

Another use of a news release is to announce that you are holding a news conference. These are covered on page 195.

Advance notices can be very short, saying only:

- What the event is.
- When.
- Where.
- What for.
- Who is involved.

Expand this, in the way explained above, if there is a news point to be made at this stage. If not, then don't waste your time or the reporters' time on more than the bare facts.

Releasing a speech

It's often worth making use of a speech by releasing it in advance to the media, as it will get a much wider audience that way.

A very short speech can go out in full. For a longer one, send a short news release explaining when and where the speech is being made and covering the main points. If the speech is important, attach a full copy of it. Put on top of the news release the words, 'Check against Delivery'. This means that if the speaker changes what he or she is going to say, but the journalist has not waited for the speech and so printed the words originally in the news release rather than what was said, it is their responsibility. In practice, reporters very rarely do wait for the speech itself, and occasionally they get caught out as a result.

Releasing a publication

If you are publishing something that you want to be noticed in the media, you need to give the journalists time to read it themselves! So set a publication date, and send out free media copies with a news release beforehand. State what the publication date is and ask them not to print anything before that date.

A long report that is fairly newsworthy, but is never going to make it onto the front page, probably needs ten days or a fortnight. A short report, or one that is going to be controversial, needs less time. With something that is really 'hot' or that involves a leak of sensitive or confidential material, give no more than 24 hours' notice. Any longer, and the journalists will be itching to break the embargo. The chances of rumours reaching the wrong people will also increase.

Sending out media copies can be expensive, so limit them to the people who you think will use the story. It is generally a waste of time to send out news releases to the national papers without attaching the publications as well – they won't be used. The local papers may do so, though.

The media expect to get their copies of publications for free, so include the cost of this in your budget. Once a news story has appeared, you may get other requests for copies from journalists you had not thought of contacting. When you run out of free copies, answer any extra requests with a polite letter saying that you have done so and giving details of where they can buy one. But be flexible: if someone really important suddenly wants a copy, send one out of the stock you were planning to sell.

'Placing' a story

One way to get extra coverage for a report or publication is to 'place' it with a specialist magazine, and then work with them on publicity. To do this, you need to make contact with the editor several months before the date on which you expect to release the story generally, and to let them have it on an exclusive basis. They might be willing to do a feature on the subject, or to invite you to contribute an article. They can then send out a news release themselves about the story. This benefits them by publicising the magazine, and you by getting more coverage. So it is worth spending a substantial amount of time setting up and working on this sort of cooperative deal.

Photographs

Most stories in the newspapers and magazines are accompanied by photographs, either of the individual concerned or of something that illustrates the point. You can send a photograph with a news release, as suggested on page 200. More often, the editor will want to arrange his/her own pictures.

Photographers tend to be overworked and not very interested in the story, only in taking the pictures and going away. They will probably phone for an appointment at fairly short notice, turn up with all their equipment, take a dozen photographs and go off.

Try to get the photographs taken against a background that suits your story and your image. Don't let yourselves be 'set up' with what suits the media's idea of you. There are some ideas about this on page 213.

If you are running an event, such as a public meeting or a carnival, news photographers may again turn up. They could want you to pose specially rather than simply taking photographs as events go on. It will usually be in your interests to agree to this, as they can create a better picture for you in this way. For instance, if you have a celebrity attending, it will be worth arranging a photo of him/her shaking hands with the group secretary. Try to get the group's logo, or a slogan, into every photograph.

Most local newspapers sell prints of photos that have appeared in the paper, and it will be worth getting copies of these to display. If you want to reproduce them – for instance in your annual report – you must ask permission. You may need to pay a reproduction fee as well. See Chapter 10, on copyright laws, for more details about this.

18
Talking to the media

This Chapter deals with meeting people from the press, TV and radio face to face and on the phone; being photographed; being interviewed on TV and radio.

Whether you are talking to a reporter on the phone, meeting them in the pub, or being interviewed in the full glare of television lights, the effect is the same. You are on show, and through you your whole group or organisation. The image that the public will see is the result of the image that the media take away from you, and that they pass on to the public. So if you want to give yourself the chance to come over well, you *must*:

- know what you are doing, or what you are talking about; and
- come over as reasonable and friendly.

It is rather as if you are applying for a job, each time you speak to a reporter for five minutes. You've got only those minutes to make a good impression, and so you must put your best foot forward.

Always prepare for your contacts with the media, whether you are taking the initiative or they are. Put yourself in the shoes of the reporter, and think what s/he will want to know. What will make the story more interesting for the readers, viewers or listeners?

Make clear what is fact and what is your opinion. If there's something you don't know, say so and offer to find out and contact them again with the answer. Follow that up quickly – or if you can't find out, phone and say that instead, with apologies.

If possible, put together a media pack that you can send or give any journalist who contacts you. When you know what they are particularly interested in, add details of addresses, other contacts, books or reports they could read. Check through some of these yourself, to make sure you understand the background fully. Jot down, or photocopy, the most important facts and figures.

Many of the questions from reporters will be very basic, because they will be checking that they have understood the point you are making, and have the facts right. So you might get asked:

191

- What your organisation is, what it does, and why.
- Who's involved in it, and where it gets its money from.
- More details about the point of the news release or the event.
- What you'd say to people opposing you, or putting alternative arguments.

Sound confident and as if you believe in the subject when you talk to a reporter. It will make them believe in you too.

The reporter may give you a hard time and test the opposition arguments on you. If s/he is a specialist or has already spoken to other experts, you may find the questions quite searching. If there is a strong point you genuinely hadn't thought of, admit it rather than flounder on looking silly.

Most reporters are looking for information to help them write their story, rather than to catch you out or try to trick you. Even if you suspect they are being malicious or biased, treat them with courtesy and as if it is the last thing that has entered your head.

Don't let yourself be drawn by leading questions, such as the reporter saying, 'Wouldn't you agree that ...' Say instead, 'No, what I think is ...'

Always ask if you are going to be quoted by name, and ask the reporter to read back the words s/he is going to quote. If they are picking your brains as an expert on the subject, a journalist from a specialist magazine may be willing to let you see and comment on a piece before it goes to the printer. A person working for a newspaper probably will not, though. That's partly because of time problems, and partly because s/he will be worried that you'll spoil the story by picking up small pedantic points. If you do get sent a draft, look at it as soon as you can, and phone or fax your comments over quickly.

No reporter ever really goes off duty. An off the cuff comment to a friendly journalist in the pub may be followed up at the time with a request for more details, or it could be picked up later, and the story behind it investigated. So be very cautious about ever telling a reporter anything that you don't want to become public.

'Off the record'

To say that you are 'off the record' when talking to a reporter means that you are telling them something that you don't want reported. You can add a bit of background information to a story, or offer a few helpful hints 'off the record,' and this will normally be respected. But if you tell the most important and interesting part of the story in that way, then the temptation to use it may get the better of the journalist. In any case, the reporter may ferret around and ask other people until they find someone indiscreet. Alternatively, they may use the story 'unattributably' which means they don't name their source. Either way the effect is the same – the story is out. So if there is going to be trouble about it, be prepared. See Chapter 10 for the law on confidential information.

Remember to say when you are back 'on the record' again.

Phone calls

Most reporters do most of their work on the phone. You are more likely to talk to them in that way than face to face.

When you've sent out a news release, the people who should deal with the queries are the people named in the news release. But for calls that come out of the blue, you should decide on your policy in advance, and make sure the person on the switchboard, or who takes incoming calls, knows what it is.

When a journalist phones, find out first who they are and what article or programme they are working on. If it is a publication you have not heard of, ask for some details about it – who publishes it, how many people read it, where it is on sale. Make a note of the reporter's name and a contact phone number however short the conversation.

Log any media calls, on a record card or a computer database, and also note it on the contacts file. Put a brief summary of what was discussed. Find out from the reporter when the report is going to be published or broadcast, and then try to monitor it. If it is a specialist magazine, they may be willing to send you a copy.

Except for very trivial queries, it is best not to answer unexpected calls off the cuff. Find out what the reporter wants, and say that you will phone back in five minutes. Reporters normally do not mind this, so long as you keep to your word.

If you are being asked about a statement that someone else has made, or a report they have published, ask for details before making any comment. Write them down, and if they are complicated, read them back to the reporter. This will give you time to think about your comments. If you are in any doubt about whether they have got it right, contact the person or organisation, or some other source of information, to check before saying anything.

Before ringing back, jot down one or two key points, and then stick to them. Try to avoid being drawn into a general discussion. If you think the reporter has the wrong idea, or is trying to create a story where none exists, say so.

See Chapter 7 for general points about communicating on the phone.

If you are asked to do an interview for the radio or television on the phone, treat it just as you would an interview in a studio, covered on pages 209–12.

Managing a crisis

If there is a crisis and you are being flooded with calls, you may want to give several people in your office a prepared statement, and ask them to read it out to any media people who phone. Stress that they must not make any comment beyond it; tell them to suggest that the person concerned rings back later if they want to speak to the media officer personally.

It is unwise to say, 'No comment,' or to refuse to speak to the media. It can be made to look as if you have something to hide. Instead, draft a short statement saying very little, such as, 'The matter is under active discussion and an announcement will be made as soon as possible.' Go on repeating this, in a polite way, for as long as you are under pressure.

If there are a lot of calls and it is disturbing your work or home life, you could call a news conference (explained on page 195). You would then be able to say, 'I can't comment now, but if you come to the news conference at 3pm, you will have the chance to ask questions.' You do, though, need to have something of substance to announce in that case. You'll be given a rough time if you are simply stonewalling.

Chapter 21 explains what action you can take, and how you can complain, if you are harassed or misrepresented by the media.

Meeting a reporter

You could be meeting a reporter personally as part of a series of informal contacts (covered in the last Chapter) or for a particular reason. If they ask for the meeting, try to find out what is behind it. Why do they want to meet you rather than anyone else? Ask who they have met already.

Go with something to say, or something you want to find out from them. If you pursue that point firmly, you will be less likely to get drawn into saying things that you did not intend or don't mean.

Wear clothes that are neat, clean, and reasonably smart. Make sure the rest of your appearance fits in with them. It could be better not to fit too closely with the media's image of your sort of organisation. The spokeswoman for a women's aid group, for instance, would do better to wear a dress and tights when meeting the media, rather than dungarees covered with badges. The dungarees could lead to her being written off as 'one of those women's libbers,' before she had even opened her mouth.

Try to arrange the meeting in a place where you will feel at ease. Your workplace or your home may be the best place, but only if it is going to give the right impression. This could mean a frantic tidying up, and perhaps also taking down posters and stickers from the walls. Otherwise try a *quiet* pub or cafe, or something like the entrance to a public meeting – the local library, community centre, or Town Hall.

Be careful about alcohol. Whatever the circumstances of your meeting, stick to the soft and low-alcohol drinks. Even the hardest-headed person will talk more excitably, and arrange their thoughts less clearly, after a drink or two. Many people are prone to say things that they don't mean, or in a way that they regret afterwards. Lavish lunches can have the same effect, so if you are offered hospitality, suggest somewhere modest where you won't be overawed by the surroundings.

Holding a news conference

This will only occasionally be the right thing for a campaigning group to do. Most of the time, the media will be too busy to attend. But the times when it is useful are:

- When you know that you will have a major piece of news to announce, which is likely to go into national newspapers and news programmes. The start or finish of a big industrial dispute, for instance, might justify setting up a news conference.

- When you are being pestered by the media over a particular issue, and want to fend them off.

- When you have a major celebrity or personality under your wing, and you want to give the media the opportunity to ask questions. You could set up a conference instead of individual interviews, or only give the interviews to one or two people, and tell the rest to come to your conference.

The advantage of a news conference is that *you* can set the agenda, if you are well prepared and professional.

Setting the conference up

If you have a meeting room on your premises, which is tidy and not shabby, you could use that. Otherwise, book a smallish room in a hotel, the Civic Centre, or a similar place. It's better to have people crowding in the space at the back, than to have acres of empty chairs. Make sure the room is well-lit, and has several electric plugs. Try to find one that is easily accessible, with parking. If there is time, send a map out with the invitation.

Arrange the conference for the morning, around 11.00 or 11.30, so that the journalists can meet their deadlines. Aim for it to last about an hour, but book the room for an hour beforehand to allow for getting it ready, and an hour afterwards. Provide coffee and biscuits, before and afterwards, and say you are doing so on the invitation.

Don't offer drinks or a buffet, unless the conference is going to run over lunchtime. Journalists do not expect campaigning groups to provide lavish hospitality, and they could look askance at you if you did.

Arrange the chairs in rows, if possible behind tables, so that the journalists can rest their notepads or portable computers on them. Leave space at the sides and back, especially if you are expecting a television crew, as they will need room to set up lights and move around.

Set out chairs and a table at the front for the speakers. Cover the front of the table with posters about your organisation, or drape your banner along it, and put posters up on the wall behind the speakers. Put them at a height where anyone taking a picture of the speaker will include them in it. Move away, or cover up, anything that is going to look unsightly behind the speakers, like a patch of damp on the wall or a torn curtain. Make the speakers' table look good – a bowl of flowers works wonders. The speakers should look good too. The men need to wear collars and ties, the women neat dresses or blouses. If you have a badge or a sticker about your campaign, ask everyone to wear them. Your stewards, but not your speakers, could also wear the campaign T-shirt if you have one.

Make name badges for your speakers: buy some blank badges from a stationer's, cut up your notepaper and glue your logo or the group's name on each badge, and write each person's name clearly underneath it.

Get two or three people to act as stewards, and identify them clearly with a badge or armband. One person should sit behind a table at the entrance, with a list of all those invited, and check them off as they come in. Write their names and who they represent on a sticky label with a felt tip, and ask them to wear it. Explain that this will help the Chair identify them when they ask a question.

Give each reporter a media pack. This should consist of:

- A copy of the news release you are issuing.
- A transcript of the full speeches being made.
- Material about your organisation and your campaign – such as the Annual Report, leaflets, brochures, and campaign newspapers.

Put all these in a clear plastic or card folder. Keep a few spares, to give to people who turn up without having told you in advance.

If people from TV and radio arrive, assign one of the stewards to look after them. S/he should check what facilities they need for their equipment. Offer them the chance of an interview afterwards with your main speaker, in a separate room if possible.

Aim to start the conference at the time given on the invitation, even if there are very few people there. They may well be running on a tight timetable, with a deadline to meet or another appointment.

The format to use

Appoint one of your representatives as Chair. His or her task is to introduce the others, select the people to ask questions and stop anyone going on too long, and wind up the proceedings when enough information has been given or you have run out of time. The Chair should be a different person from the main keynote speaker.

This person might be the head of your organisation, or the celebrity you have invited the reporters to meet, or the controversial figure they are after. The main points – the reasons for calling the conference – should be highlighted in that keynote speech. They also need highlighting in your news release. There might also be other speakers to expand on particular points. Don't let anyone go on too long. At most, the keynote speech should be about ten minutes, and other speeches considerably shorter.

The media officer and all those it affects in the group should know in advance what the speakers are going to say. They should be briefed not to stray beyond what has been put into the media pack. Try to think in advance about what questions might be asked, including hostile ones, and decide what the answers should be. It's acceptable to say politely, 'I've nothing to add to my previous answer,' or 'I can't give you any further information on that point,' or to repeat what you have already said, in different words.

Part of the Chair's job is to get the speaker off the hook if s/he is being pressed too hard by a journalist. The Chair could say, for instance, 'Now you've heard what X has to say, and that s/he has nothing to add to the previous answer. Can we move on to the next question, please?'

Both Chair and speakers should rehearse beforehand. Check the speeches are of the right length, establish the order in which people are going to speak, and practise responding to questions from the floor.

At the end, the Chair should thank everyone for attending, offer them further coffee, and perhaps give them the chance to meet the speakers or other members of the group informally. But while there is a single reporter still in the room, your organisation is still on show and the reporters are still on duty. Any comments made to their departing backs could be reported. They might even turn back to investigate what they had overheard.

Afterwards, check who has attended. Phone any of the missing ones who you consider important to ask if they would like to know what has been said. Offer to send them a media pack – by a messenger that day, if necessary – or at least to fax over a news release.

News conferences in a crisis

If there is a major crisis, or if your organisation is suddenly big news, you can forget most of the rules. You may need to hold the news conference at midnight, on the steps of the factory or your office. But some things remain essential even in this case. They are:

- Your speakers should look respectable, in the conventional sense of being tidy and neatly dressed.
- They should speak from a prepared note, and have an idea of the response to give to questions.
- Someone should take the chair and keep the meeting under control.

When your meeting or action finishes, don't go out immediately to face the media. Give yourselves ten minutes or a quarter of an hour to tidy yourselves up, and decide what you are going to say and who will say it. It is usually better to stick to one speaker in these cases, but you may want others to add certain points. People must not chip in without it having been agreed beforehand, though, as they may spoil the picture you are trying to put over.

The reporters should be given something on paper to take away with them. It need not be a formal news release written in the way outlined on pages 179–81, if there is no time for that. It could simply be a series of quotes from what your speaker has said, repeating the main points that have been made and giving any figures. Prepare this in your short meeting beforehand, send someone away to type it up and photocopy it, and hand it out to the reporters as they leave.

Try a big hotel, or the offices of another campaigning group or a trade union, if you need access to a typewriter or photocopier out of hours. If you can't find these in the time available, tell the reporters you will be sending on a news release as soon as possible, and take the opportunity to polish it a little more.

Photo-opportunities

The media love a photo-opportunity, an event or activity that is going to provide a good picture, preferably one that tells the story. The stock phrase is that, 'a picture is worth a thousand words.' So if you can arrange things to create that picture, you are likely to get extra coverage. This will be more likely if there are no other events in the area which are getting their own coverage, so try to ensure that the date you pick does not clash with someone else's event. The main library locally may keep a diary of events, or there may be a free, 'What's on' publication. You could also ask any of the local reporters with whom you are on friendly terms about what is in their news diary.

There is a fine line between creating opportunities for pictures, and running cheap stunts for the sake of publicity. Consider, when you are deciding whether an activity is suitable or not:

- Does it add to the image of your organisation that you are trying to get across to the public, or reduce it?
- Does it help to get across the message you are trying to put over?
- Will people be able to understand the point you are making, if a newspaper prints only a picture with a one-sentence caption underneath?

So anything you set up must be *relevant*, easy to understand and self-contained. You need a short clear slogan on badges and banners very close to the action (so that they get into the photograph) and a message which can be translated into a picture.

There are many ways in which you can turn a fairly straightforward action into an event with a little imagination. For example, the news release on page 184 refers to the Elmbank Action Group presenting a petition. They could:

- Have school children doing the presentation.
- Draw a giant map of the streets affected, print the words of the petition at the top in large letters. They could then hold this behind the councillor and the person handing the petition as the photos are taken.
- Bring along pictures or replicas of the things they want installed, like a piece of guard rail or a model of a traffic island, and present these along with a petition.

Children, animals, people in recognisable uniforms – like ambulance workers or nurses – all make good pictures. So do big name celebrities. Give them something to do or hold that illustrates your message. Without that, it will turn into a picture of the celebrity rather than of the message.

Activities that make people look undignified – especially politicians or professionals – can work well, so long as it is with their full consent. But activities that would be seen as in bad taste or might alarm people if they did not realise that they were a stunt, like a mock kidnapping or bank raid, could backfire.

Events that have been used time and again, but will still probably get some interest from the local if not the national media, are:

- Presenting a giant cheque to someone, to demonstrate how much money has been collected, how much has been lost, or how much is needed before something is done.

- A group towing a bus, or pushing a bed down a main street. Decorate it with your slogan, pictures illustrating your demands, and the group's logo.

- A football match or tug of war as a way of raising money for your cause, with a local 'name' kicking off or blowing the whistle. Have everyone in T-shirts with your slogan on, and put banners all round the ground also with your slogan and your logo.

Look through back issues of your local papers (in a library or the newspaper office) and see what sort of events they have covered in the past. Add your own twist so that the event is not too close a copy.

Prepare and rehearse your event. Plan well in advance, decide what props you need, and put one person in charge of collecting them. Work out what it is going to cost, and give that person a budget. If your plans are going to take you out of doors, decide what to do if it's raining.

Tell the media exactly what you are going to do, where you will be, and at what time, and then stick to it. Phone round the day before, to see who is likely to be coming. Prepare a news release explaining what you are trying to highlight, and why. Take it with you to hand to those who attend, together with any background material. Get people together in advance, and check that they all know what their roles are, and what order the event goes in. Send someone on in advance to meet and look after the media that turn up. Then the rest of you should arrive as a group, a few minutes early but not so much that you stand around looking silly.

If there are any reporters there at the time you have given, stage your event then so that they can leave. If others are expected but have not arrived, stay around afterwards, and send someone to telephone to see if they are coming. If they arrive then, stage your event again for their benefit. Stay smiling and good-humoured, even if you are cold and they seem to want endless retakes. The media officer, or whoever is in charge for this event, should make sure that the photographers don't manoeuvre you into providing pictures you *don't* want in the papers.

One of your group should have a camera with them, and take pictures. Get the film developed that day. Then phone the reporters who did not attend, and offer copies of the news release and the pictures. Most newspapers prefer large black and white prints, so try to fit in with that.

Even if no one turns up and there is no coverage, your activity need not be wasted. Use the photos yourselves in your publicity material – in leaflets and posters, in the Annual Report, with later news releases hammering home the same message. You may also be able to use the same props again, in different locations or in a different way.

You might want to video the event for showing elsewhere. See Chapter 15 for this. But there's no point in offering this to the media, as the quality of home video equipment is much poorer than the equipment they use – though this may change.

After you've had publicity

Keep a scrapbook or file of copies of newspaper cuttings that feature your group. Write the name of the newspaper or magazine, and the publication date, on each cutting. Use photocopies of the newspaper cuttings in leaflets, in your Annual Report, and in packs of background material you send out to journalists and potential supporters. Keep copies of cuttings about the issue you are concerned over as well.

Keeping the scrapbook is a task that can be allocated to one person, separately from the media officer. S/he may need a budget, if it means buying extra newspapers and magazines.

You can use one sort of publicity to generate another. For instance, if someone in your group writes an article in a specialist magazine setting out your ideas, or your organisation is featured in one of the quality newspapers, that in itself will be news for your local newspapers or TV and radio. Produce a news release about it as soon as possible, and send a copy of the relevant piece with it.

Keep an eye on the letters page of the newspapers in which you have been reported, to see if you have provoked a response. A good reply will keep your name in the public eye, and give you a chance to put across your point again. See Chapter 19 for ideas about writing letters to newspapers.

19

Letters to newspapers and advertisements

The letters page

In local newspapers, the letters page is one of the most widely read. In the national ones also, and in magazines, almost everyone glances at it. If they see a name they know, or the letter is about something that interests them, they will probably read it. People often remember letters better than news stories.

So that makes the letters page well worth using. However, don't try to exploit it too much. If the editor suspects there is an organised letter writing campaign on a particular subject, s/he may decide not to print any more letters on that subject. Letters putting forward controversial views can sometimes also be counter-productive. If your letter encourages the editor to accept contradictory letters or make a riposte, you could end up generating more hostile coverage than if you had left well alone. The risk of this is probably greatest when you are going against the newspaper's declared policy. So you need to think carefully whether this is the best method.

You can use letters when:

- There's a national or local event, or piece of news, that you can link with to make the issue seem topical. You could write about almost anything just before or after a Budget, for instance, or before or after the local Council announced its plans for next year. If there's a major campaign or industrial dispute going on in the area, the editor will probably take several letters about the issue.

- To take up comments made by someone else, if they make a point that you want to reinforce. You may be able to do this more than once, though eventually the editor will say, 'This correspondence is now closed'.

Check the date by which a letter has to be received in order to be printed in the next edition. It's best to write as soon as possible after the event or story you are following up.

Writing a letter

Writing a letter for the newspapers is much like writing a good news release. It needs to be short, clear, and to the point. The first sentence should sum up the reason you are writing, and link back to the news story or other letter that has prompted you to write. So you could start, 'Mr X's letter of [date] has highlighted just how far we are lagging behind our European colleagues ...' or, 'Yet again, in the Budget of last week, the Chancellor showed how little he cared for ...'

Then go on to expand the point you are making, in as few words as possible, and sum up in a single sentence at the end.

Some people have a talent for very short witty letters, just one sentence long. The best of them make a serious point in a funny way, and they are remembered. So if one of your group has this skill, persuade him or her to make use of it. But avoid irony and sarcasm, as they are risky unless done very well. Other people may take the words at face value and miss the point you are making.

Decide, before you write the letter, whether you are writing as a representative of the group, or as an individual. If you are writing as a representative, make this clear in the text of the letter itself, and also put your official position after your signature. Writing officially could add weight to what you are saying. But if you want to make it plain that there is a ground swell of opinion on a particular subject, it will be better to ask several group members to write in as individuals, each making a different point.

Don't write anonymously unless there is a good reason. Always make it clear, in the text of the letter, what that is. So for instance, you might say, 'I cannot give my name because if I do, I will lose my job'. Put your name and address in a covering letter to the editor, explaining the position, and put at the bottom of the letter the words, 'Name and address supplied.' Most editors will not print a letter that is sent to them without a name being supplied. They will, though, respect a request not to print the name.

Advertising

Advertising in the media can be expensive. If it is done in the right place, it can be cost effective also. To get value for money, it usually needs to be done in conjunction with other parts of a publicity campaign, or as a lead-up to something else.

You can use advertising for:

• Telling people a local event is happening. The Events pages of local newspapers are heavily read. If you are having a jumble sale, a social event, or an open day, put an advertisement in the papers that circulate in the immediate area of your event. Most people won't travel very far.

- Drawing attention to a national event – perhaps a demonstration or a fund-raising show. You can advertise it in the national papers or magazines, though this is expensive. Use mainly the ones your supporters read. The people to whom your advertisement will be most useful will be those who were thinking vaguely of turning up, but were not sure of the time and place.

- Drawing attention to the issue, and to gain funds and supporters. The big national charities and campaigning groups often run advertisements of this sort, especially in papers such as *The Guardian*. Sometimes their advertisements pay for themselves directly, in terms of the new supporters and donations they bring. In other cases, the response is poor, but the organisations think it is worthwhile to continue because it keeps them in the public eye. They believe that people will give more readily to street collections or other appeals as a result. This argument is rather doubtful, and an organisation which is strapped for cash will probably do better not to continue with a newspaper advertising campaign which is not paying its way.

- To show that there is a lot of support among 'important' people for a particular issue. This is quite a popular activity nowadays, especially when groups are trying to establish themselves. Collecting the signatures, though, is very time-consuming. Most will need both a letter and a follow-up phone call or discussion. It does mean that those people are then committed, and you can probably use them in other ways also, such as fundraising.

- Telling people about a publication, like a book or a pamphlet. This will be most effective in a specialist magazine read by the people who are going to be most interested in the subject.

- Putting over your case as part of a national campaign, or in response to someone else's campaign. Big national organisations such as the TUC have done this at times, to answer government advertising or publicity campaigns on issues like the Health Service. It costs a lot of money, as to make an impact you need to take full or half-page spreads in all the national papers on the same day. This then becomes news in its own right, and you can exploit it by trying to arrange to appear on programmes like *Today* to put your case in more detail.

Whatever sort of advertising you are doing, decide first who you want to reach, and where they are likely to see the advertisements. Put together a rough sketch of the sort of advertisement you want – thinking particularly about its size, the number of words, and any graphics or pictures. Decide also how often you want it to appear, and where. Different pages have different prices. The back cover and inside front cover of a magazine are the most expensive, or the front page and first four pages of a newspaper. Then find out what it will cost to put it together, and have it printed in the place that will serve your purpose best. It's worth asking about discounts for 'good causes', or any special deals. Just at present (early 1992) there is heavy discounting by most papers and magazines, because they are very short of advertising, so it will be worth trying to bargain over the figure they quote you. If you are prepared to take a chance about where they put the advertisement, you may be able to get it cheaper. There might also be a discount for settling your account quickly, or for putting advertisements in particular editions. Local papers often have several titles in a group, and the rates will vary depending on which one your advertisements are to go into.

If you find that the cost is too high, cut the number of publications you are advertising in or the number of times it appears, rather than reduce the size or lessen the appearance of the advertisement. The money is only well spent if it makes an impact.

Advertisements are sold in column inches, in centimetres or in fractions of a page. Newspapers each have a standard layout including columns which are a certain size across. You buy the width of one column or more, and the length that you want. There are normally a number of standard sizes, though they can be varied if you want. Alternatively, you can have a full, half or quarter page. There's also usually a difference in price between 'display' advertisements (with a box drawn round them) and those without. It is worth paying the extra for display advertisements, as they stand out much more.

Many newspapers and magazines have a box on one of their papers giving details of their advertising rates and terms. If you can't find this, phone the advertising manager at their office number. In any case, phone before placing an advertisement, and check such points as:

- The dates by which you must supply the advertisements.
- Whether they can be in draft, or must be camera ready (explained on page 83).
- What form any graphics, photos or other artwork must be in (see Chapter 9, on printing, for an explanation of the various forms);
- Whether they will let you have proofs to check before printing, if they are producing the advertisements.
- Who you should be liaising with, and who to contact if there are any problems.

Make a note of what has been agreed, and check it against the publisher's estimate or the invoice when it arrives.

Design

If your newspaper or magazine advertising is a major part of your campaign, and you are going in the leading pages, it will be worth going to professionals – an advertising agency or a design group – for the design work. It is almost essential in national and large-circulation papers and magazines. Every other advertiser will have gone to the professionals, so an amateur advertisement will stick out like a sore thumb.

You may be able to find an advertising or design person who will do the work for free. See pages 41–2 for more details on this, and ideas on points to watch.

If you are planning a steady stream of advertising – even in smaller publications – it will be worth paying for one design job, creating a standard layout for your advertisement, using your logo and a particular typeface and style. You will then be able to re-use it with different words, announcing events or publications in future. Alter it after a year or so, though, because it will become stale and people will think they have already seen the advertisement and no longer read it.

Your design should be clear and clean-looking. Keep the number of images, and words and graphics, to a minimum. The best advertisements, in the commercial world, are those with a single striking image, or slogan, or both, and then an explanation in the text. The picture and slogan should draw people on to read the text, as briefly as possible.

If money is not a problem, you can include a lot of words in the text. As you will see in the national papers, this is often done with full page spreads. For the sort of group reading this book, though, money *is* likely to be a problem, and it's better to make a virtue of necessity and keep the number of words down, rather than crowd too many into a small space. Follow the rules of communication set out in Chapter 3. *Always* get someone else to check over your text before it goes into the newspaper or magazine. It's very easy to leave out or misspell a word, and it will be glaringly obvious once it's published.

If you are looking for a response from the public, include a return coupon in the advertisement. People are much more likely to use this than to write you a separate letter. Code the coupon, so that you know where it has come from. That is, include, 'Dept BX,' or 'Room 253,' or something similar, in the return address, and use a different department or room number in the next advertisement. Then keep a note of where the different responses have come from. Don't use the media that bring the least responses again, unless there is some other good reason.

If your advertisement doesn't look as it should, or does not appear in the right place or on the right day, *complain*. Ask for a rebate on the cost, or for the advertisement to be reprinted correctly, at no extra charge. Think twice about using the publication again, even if it seems to have been an honest mistake. It suggests that their administration is sloppy, and that there could be other mistakes in future.

20

Going on the radio or TV

Your appearances on radio or TV are likely to be on news or feature programmes. They will probably come about because you have sent the producers a news release or invited them to an event, or because you have become 'news' in yourselves. So before you read this Chapter, look at Chapters 16–18, on dealing with the media.

TV and radio journalists are much the same as newspaper and magazine journalists, but there are some differences:

- The audience for the leading programmes is far larger than the number of readers of most newspapers. Even the smaller-audience, 'quality' programmes are seen by far more people than read the equivalent newspapers or magazines.

- Partly as a result of this, and partly because of the technical demands of radio and TV, the journalists working on them tend to be more pushy and demanding.

- TV works by seeming to be very *personal*. It creates the illusion that it is bringing us closer to real people, who therefore need to be colourful personalities. So the journalists are often looking for a human interest angle even when the issue behind the programme is very serious or abstract. This means that appearance, style and personality could be more important than knowledge or representativeness, in deciding who gets on to a programme and who does not.

Research for a programme

For TV and radio journalists, the first stage in putting together a programme is *research*. In the case of a news programme, this will often be a quick phone call or two, following up a news release or something that has appeared in the newspapers. Look at the book *News in the Regions* (details in Appendix 1: Booklist) to see how the regional programmes work. The national ones are much the same, though on a larger scale and better staffed. The phone call may come from the producer him/herself, or from a researcher. S/he will probably start by asking a few questions about the issue itself, before asking if you

207

would like to come on the programme. This is mainly to test out whether you know your subject, and can put it over to others.

With a longer feature or documentary programme, there could be several weeks' or months' research before they are ready to start recording. Some of this will be reading books and other material, but very often the main research will be by talking to people who already know about the subject.

The major programmes have full time researchers. The big names – the people who actually appear on the screen or whose voices you hear – will often not be involved until late in the process. They will be told by other people what questions to ask or issues to raise.

Researchers are mostly youngish graduates. They may not know a lot about the subject they are working on. In the small independent TV companies, they are likely to be part of a team that does everything within the company, and may well have moved from the BBC or ITV to the independent as a way of furthering their careers. They will often give the impression that they know less than they do as a way of making you talk and allowing them to pick your brains easily.

It is worth cooperating with these researchers, though it can be very time-consuming. It establishes you or your group as experts on the subject, and once you are in one researcher's address book it is likely that you will be contacted by others. It also means that you are involved in setting the agenda – that is, in sorting out the important questions that the programme should concentrate on.

If you are based near to the programme's office, they will often expect you to come and see them. But if it is some distance, or it would be difficult to get there, say so and ask them to come to you instead. Be flexible about times when you are available.

There is often something of a power struggle within production teams, between researcher, director, and producer. It is quite easy to get caught up in this as an unwitting interviewee or consultant. The researcher may make promises to you about your role, and then be overruled by the director because you don't seem right for the style of programme s/he has in mind. There is not very much you can do about this, except to be aware of it, and not to be too offended if you are suddenly dropped.

See pages 194–5 for guidelines about how to behave when meeting a journalist, and what work to do in advance.

If you become more involved

If your group is heavily involved in the research for a programme, ask for a written contract as a consultant and a fee, based on the amount of time you think you are likely to have to spend. Don't underprice yourselves. Work out your wage costs per hour, and then multiply that figure by three *at least* to cover overheads. Many of the programmes work on the basis that they give a fee when asked, but are not the first ones to mention it.

How much you will get depends partly on your negotiating skill, and partly on the company making the programme. Many of the small independents are working on very tight budgets. If you dig your heels in and insist on too much, they will simply not use you. So if you really want to be involved, be prepared to lower your sights. On the other hand, a prestige programme like *Panorama* has plenty of money, so you may as well make sure you get a reasonable proportion of it. You do not have to accept the first offer as if it is a set amount – these fees are always negotiable.

If you are being credited in the programme for research you have done, or other assistance, say in advance that you will want to approve the script before it is recorded, to check that it is something you want to put your name to. If you are unhappy, explain your reasons and try to convince them. Ultimately, you may have to say that you want your name taken off the credits. It is unlikely that you will be able to stop them putting out the programme in some form, though.

Appearing on radio or TV

If you are asked to appear on a programme, find out all you can from the person inviting you. Jane Drinkwater, in *Get it On* (see Appendix 1: Booklist) suggests the following questions:

- What is the programme?
- Who is doing the interview?
- What do they want your comments on, and what is the line of questioning likely to be?
- Will it go out to a national or local audience, and what are the estimated numbers?
- How long is your slot likely to be?
- Will it be live or recorded?
- Will there be other contributors and if so, who are they?

There will be cases where the interviewer or presenter is someone who you feel will be biased against you or hostile, or where the format will not give you a chance to put your point across. A well-handled hostile interview can do your organisation a lot of good, but it takes confidence. If you do not feel you can do it, decline politely – perhaps without giving a reason – rather than persevere with what you feel will be an unsatisfactory appearance.

Use the person in your organisation who will come over best on radio or TV, even if they are not your most senior figure. This could result in some hurt feelings, so break it to the other person gently, and suggest that they go on a training course (see page 213).

If the interview is not to be in a studio, try to get it in a place which will add to the message you are trying to put over, rather than reduce or change it. Some backgrounds give the interview extra authority, such as a desk in a book-filled room. Government ministers, for instance, usually try to get themselves filmed with shelves of government reports behind them. You can do the same, using shelves including your reports or pamphlets, or your own group's posters carrying a logo or slogan.

If they are keen to interview you outdoors, look for a background that will reinforce your message. So if you are being interviewed about unemployment, for instance, a background of a closed factory would hammer home your point. Don't allow yourselves to be set up, though. One well-known example of that was in the 'Winter of Discontent' in 1978–79, when a group of pickets allowed themselves to be filmed silhouetted against the sky, which looked threatening.

If you are worried about a particular shot, simply say that you don't think it will work, and move away.

Most of the rules for being interviewed are the same as the rules for good communication on pages 16–26, and for talking to reporters face-to-face or on the phone, in Chapter 18. Some specific points to remember are:

- Try to listen to the programme, or watch it, before you go on. Check on the presenter's style, and the general format.

- Always go *well prepared*. Even if you can usually perform well off the cuff, the cameras and recording equipment could unnerve you. Put down the main points, and any figures you want to quote, on small record cards or pieces of paper that you can hold in your hand. Glance at them as you need to, but don't be obviously reading them. Don't rustle them, especially on radio.

- Think what questions you are likely to be asked, including the hostile ones. Interviewers tend to act as devil's advocate, putting the opposite arguments to yours, or trying to pick holes in what you say. Work out what answers you would give. Practise, if possible, using a friend or colleague as an interviewer.

- Ask how long the interview is going to be, and select three or four main points you want to get across. Stick to them, even if the interviewer or the other contributors want to go off on another tack. People hearing your answers will not necessarily have registered just what the question is, so they will not realise you are not answering it. If the interview is being recorded, the question could in any case be edited out.

- If you're kept waiting in the hospitality room keep away from the alcohol, and even the tea and coffee! You can drink as much as you like afterwards, but you need to appear on the programme stone-cold sober and without a bursting bladder.

- Get there early and, if there is time, have a short discussion with the reporter or interviewer before recording starts. Give them the background to your organisation or campaign; assume that they know very little about the topic.

- Talk in ordinary language and simple sentences. Try to make your train of thought apparent to the listener, rather than jumping from point to point. Don't give answers that are just 'yes' or 'no' – explain why, briefly, each time.

Studio discussions

If you are asked to take part in a studio discussion, find out who else is going to be on the panel before agreeing to join. Almost certainly, you will be up against someone who takes the opposite view to you, with the reporter or interviewer holding the ring. Try to find out in advance what opinion the other person holds, and what his/her arguments are. When you are asked to speak, summarise your views and try not to give way to interruptions. If you are interrupted before you have got across one of your points, you could say when you get the chance to speak, 'Before I answer that, I just want to finish the point I was making earlier ...' and then do that, very briefly.

There may be people who are so extreme or unreasonable that you would not want to associate with them even in a studio. But think carefully before deciding that the audience should not hear your side of the story. You may be in a strong enough position to bargain with the programme editor, saying, 'I'll gladly take part, but not if X is involved.' Explain your reasons. If they think you have a fair point and it would not put them into too difficult a position, they may agree.

What you sound like

For a radio interview, you will probably be tested for 'sound level' and shown where to sit or stand in relation to the microphone. Ask if no one does so. Usually you need to be about six inches away. Keep your words as clear as you can, and avoid 'um' and 'ah'. Talk to the interviewer as if s/he is an ordinary person asking about something you are both interested in. Be open and friendly, rather than obsequious or prickly.

Your appearance

For TV, take care of your appearance. Look neat, and fit the image that you want to put over. Don't wear loud stripes or checks. Don't wear anything brilliant white, because the cameras don't like it. Bright red is also a problem – it tends to look garish and shimmery.

Make-up is probably a necessity for both men and women, however much you may dislike it normally. Without it, you'll look like the poor relation. You'll probably be whisked off and made-up anyway, without being asked. If this does not happen, at least wipe your face before going on the air, as you will probably be sweating from the lights and the heat.

For radio, the audience can't see you, but the people making the programme and the other participants can, so it is worth taking trouble with your appearance here too.

When the camera is there

Once you are on camera, think about what you are doing with your hands and feet, and with your body in general. Sit or stand up straight, look the reporter in the eye, and be assertive and confident. Don't wave your arms around too much, don't scratch your head or pick your nose, and don't shuffle your feet.

If you are being recorded, when you make a bad mistake, or feel that you have messed up an answer and could do it better, you can say so and ask if you can do it again. For radio, this is normally quite easy; for TV, it may be difficult to persuade them of the need, as filming is expensive. If the programme is going out live, you will just have to plough on.

With television recording, the camera team will probably take some 'establishing shots' at some point, to go in at the beginning of the piece, showing the background against which you are sitting or standing. The reporter will then say something as a lead-in to the interview. They will also record some 'cutaways,' which are shots of you just talking or listening, to fill in gaps and stop the camera seeming to jump. They may also re-record the questions or comments by the reporter, so that they can fit them in later.

Costs

If you are being filmed for a feature, ask for your travelling expenses and other financial losses (such as childcare) to be met. Always ask them to send a taxi to pick you up and to take you home, at their expense. Even if you have your own transport available, this will be much more relaxing than trying to find your way, be on time, and look for a parking space.

If a TV crew uses your premises or your home for filming, you should be given a 'facility fee,' to cover the disruption they cause, the cups of coffee you make them, and so on. They should also pay separately for any damage they do. Again, you will need to ask, as they are unlikely to volunteer.

This is especially important if the filming is taking place in the home of someone who has agreed to be used as an 'example' – perhaps a claimant or a tenant on a bad estate. The group's media officer ought to take on the negotiating role, rather than leave it to the individual being filmed. If someone is on a low income, you will need either to insist on this, or to establish that the group itself will see s/he is not out of pocket.

When you are filmed for a news programme and you are part of the news, you are less likely to get any of these things, but it is still worth trying if you have gone to a lot of trouble.

If you feel you are being treated unfairly

Say so at the time, and explain why. If you leave it to the end to complain, it could be edited out.

Stay calm and reasonable. Keep your temper, even if the reporter, or another contributor, is being provocative. Don't get caught up in a slanging match. Go on repeating what you have said already, sounding friendly about it. Don't sound sarcastic or hostile – it will alienate your audience. Rather than flatly contradict someone, use a phrase like, 'That's a very interesting issue, but ...' and then go on to say firmly why you disagree.

If you are being pressed to answer a direct question, do so, because otherwise you will sound evasive. Be wary, though, of being drawn into committing yourself to a firm position that could be quoted out of context against you. You might want to say that you will consider doing this or that, rather than that you definitely will do so.

When the 'cut-away' shots (see page 212) are being filmed, listen to the questions or comments from the interviewer. If you feel they have altered them unfairly, protest. If necessary, shout, 'That's unfair,' over the sound of his or her voice. They then won't be able to use that recording, and you can then say what you think is wrong.

See Chapter 21 for ideas on what to do if you have to complain, or even take legal action about a programme.

Training

There is now a lot of media training around, especially for TV and radio interviews. If you are likely to be doing a considerable amount of media work, it will be worth going on a short course. They can be expensive, but are worth it. For trade unionists, the TUC puts on some very good residential courses on communications and working with the media. Campaigning groups that are branches of a bigger organisation may find that their head offices run courses, or could be persuaded to put one on. Otherwise, see if the local Council for

Voluntary Service, or a similar group, will put a course on, or arrange one yourselves and get other people to join in. There is a list of some of the organisations that provide this training in Appendix 2: Addresses.

If a course given by professionals is not possible, then at least get someone to film you with a video camera, or tape your voice, doing a mock interview with someone else, to check how you look or sound. This is very easy and surprisingly helpful.

Spin offs

Make good use of your appearance or involvement in a programme. For instance:

- You might be able to issue a news release several days in advance, to the local media or to the specialist magazines, saying that you are going to be appearing and why. But it is important to check with the programme editor first about what you can say. They may want to be first with the news, and they could drop you altogether if the story leaks out in advance.

- You might instead be allowed to issue a news release embargoed for the time the programme is going out (see page 183 for what this means), including quotes from what you or others on the programme are saying. Again, check with the programme editor about this. S/he could be putting out a news release and would not want you to cut across it.

- Alternatively, you could suggest to some of the newspapers or magazines on your contact list that they might like to do a follow-up feature about it, looking at the story in more depth or from a new angle.

Ask the editor for a copy of the programme, or get someone to tape it and use it within your organisation. This then gives you a very cheap way of creating a video for your organisation. Ask for permission to use it in this way, as the copyright normally belongs to the programme makers. If you have taken a substantial part in it, though, they will probably be sympathetic. You could then show it at public meetings, or to new members and staff, or lend it out to other groups. See pages 158–9 for points on the distribution of videos.

Make use of the fact that you have been recorded in your publicity material, both before and after the event. You could issue a leaflet or newsletter in advance, telling people to watch or listen; issue another leaflet reminding them what was said (perhaps including a picture of the presenter) and then refer back to the programme again in more publicity weeks or months later, reminding them once more and telling them how the story has continued.

If your organisation has been particularly highlighted, or your project has been filmed, you could put a band across the front of a leaflet or a poster a strapline with the words, 'As seen on TV programme ...' for as long as you think people will recall it.

Finally, don't forget to include mention of the programme, and of any resulting publicity, in your Annual Report.

Phone-ins

Anyone can take part in a phone-in on the radio, whether an expert or not. You can use them to put forward an opinion, to react to the ideas that someone else is putting forward, to plug your organisation or your campaign. You can put your point in your own words, though the presenter may be able to put a different slant on them by the way s/he responds.

It is easier to get heard in the phone-in programmes run by local radio stations than it is to find a place on the national ones. But if you have something to say, it is worth trying the national ones as well.

Listen to at least one edition of the programme before you start phoning yourself. Make a note of the sort of points that are made, of the way the presenter reacts, and of how long people are given. Before you pick up the phone, jot down what you want to say in two or three sentences. Think about what sort of responses you will get.

When you get through, you'll be answered by an assistant who will ask what you want to say, and either put you on hold or ring back as soon as the slot is free. Stay in the the room while waiting for them to ring back – they will let the phone ring only a few times and then try someone else. When you get on the air, follow the guidelines on pages 209–11 for TV and radio interviews. Sometimes you may feel that they are trying deliberately to get you flustered. Don't let them succeed: it is only going to last a minute or two, and you can have a stiff drink afterwards.

Being the guest on a phone-in programme – the one being questioned – is tough. Do your homework, and write down a few important points – especially figures, if you have difficulty remembering them – on small index cards that you can spread across the table in front of you. Listen hard to what each person is saying, and note down their names. Try not to jump to conclusions from the first few words s/he says. If you are being asked for advice and don't know the answer, say so rather than inventing something. Suggest somewhere else for the person to go, such as the Citizens Advice Bureau. If the facts someone is telling you appear to be wrong, there is probably some essential point which they have left out because they don't realise its importance. You don't have time to probe much for further details, so hedge your bets, and again suggest they go somewhere else for further details.

Above all, stay polite. However obnoxious someone is being, remember that a put-down by you, in your position as celebrity, will come over as heavy and humiliating. People who might share your opinions will react against it, and feel sorry for the person you are rude to. By all means tell people firmly that they are wrong, but don't play into their hands by being offensive.

Being in a TV or radio audience

Being part of the audience in a programme such as *Question Time* or *Any Questions* is much the same as joining in a phone-in. You have only a moment to get your point in, so you must make the best of it by being brief and clear. You can also influence the atmosphere of the programme, by clapping loudly when someone has said something you support, or staying silent in opposition. Heckling a speaker on one of these programmes is *not* effective. Many politicians have a practised line in dealing with hecklers, and that is what the audience remember. In other cases it may simply sound rude. So only shout out or boo if the remark is so appalling you feel you can do nothing else.

If you are there as supporter, or as opposition, dress neatly and conventionally. Untidy, eccentric-looking people will give the viewers an image of your cause as untidy and eccentric as well.

21

Taking action against the media

This Chapter looks at what you can do when the media make a nuisance of themselves, abuse you, or misrepresent the facts.

Most journalists are reasonable human beings. They are trying to do their jobs, without enough time to carry them through properly. They are working on limited information, with an editor, and perhaps also an advertising manager, breathing down their necks. In local newspapers, radio and TV they are often inexperienced, as the local media are the first stages in most journalists' careers.

So it is important not to overreact. Things that go wrong will often be straightforward mistakes, or the result of carelessness. A simple complaint, made firmly and politely, may be enough. But if you have to complain, take the first steps quickly, preferably within two or three days of the event.

If you are misrepresented or misquoted

When there has been coverage of you or your group, check it for accuracy. Don't worry about minor errors and small differences in the slant that is put on things. But always follow up major mistakes or misquotes. Ask for a correction and apology in the same paper or magazine, otherwise it could be repeated elsewhere. Journalists usually start their research by asking their office library for the 'cuttings file,' or by going through one of the computer databases on a particular subject. They will then often recycle the material from there, only re-checking or adding to the information where they have to. So a news report with a mistake in it could be picked up by another journalist.

First, write down a few words explaining what is wrong, and draft the wording you want used to correct it. Put it in language an ordinary person can understand. Decide what you are asking for. Possibilities are:

- a correction and apology on the same page as the original mistake, or
- on a different page, but still in a place where people will see it; or

- agreement that the editor will print a letter from you, setting the facts straight, and say beneath it that s/he accepts your version and apologises; or

- agreement that they will print an article by you of at least the same length as the original one, together with a note that the editor accepts your version and apologies.

There is no legal 'right of reply' in this country. How successful you are will depend on how bad the error was, your evidence that they have got it wrong, and what power you have.

Keep these points in mind when you complain:

- Stay polite all the time.
- Don't say or write anything that might be considered libellous or slanderous (explained on pages 106–9). If writs start flying, you might find they are coming in your direction as well.
- Keep copies of letters and notes of any conversations. If you have to take things further, these will be your evidence.

Making the complaint

Contact the editor of the paper, either by phone or letter, and say that you are complaining about the journalist who wrote the story. If s/he spoke to you and has quoted you wrongly, ask for his/her notes of your conversation. Journalists are supposed to keep their notes for several years, in proper notebooks. In practice, they will often scribble on the back of an envelope and throw it away afterwards. If the notes don't exist, then it is your word against the journalist's. But if they do still have their notes, ask them to read them back to you. If you believe they do not reflect what you actually said, again it is going to be your word against the journalist's. But if they are accurate and the article does not reflect them, then you have strong grounds for complaint.

If the journalist did not speak to you, but printed wrong information, ask where s/he obtained it, and why it was not properly checked before publishing. The response may be that they tried to contact you but you were unavailable, or that they checked with another person they considered reliable. You may need to do some investigation yourself. Were there phone messages to your home or workplace which were not passed on to you? Did this other person receive a call, and if so what did s/he say? Was s/he in a position to say anything on behalf of your organisation, or was the journalist justified in believing s/he was?

If it seems by now that an honest mistake has been made, rather than a deliberate misrepresentation, treat it this way. Say that you feel it was a mistake, but that it is harming your organisation, and you would like a correction printed. This is more likely to be effective than accusing the reporter of malice, when the editor will feel bound to defend his/her employee.

If you are getting nowhere, then if you are part of a larger organisation it may be worth getting somewhere from higher up to take up the issue. A newspaper editor may shrug off the complaint of a local union branch, for instance, but want to placate the same union's Regional Secretary, who gives him or her regular stories.

The newspapers which are least likely to make mistakes, the qualities, are also the ones most likely to print a correction and and apology, because they value their reputations. The further down the scale you go, the more difficult it is likely to become. The only consolation is that readers are also becoming steadily less likely to believe what these papers say.

If pressure on the paper does not succeed, you have the choice of either dropping the matter, or going to an outside body with your complaint. Possibilities are:

- Complaining to the National Union of Journalists.
- In the case of the national daily and Sunday newspapers, complaining to the paper's ombudsman.
- Complaining to the Press Complaints Commission or the Broadcasting Complaints Commission.
- Taking legal action for libel or slander.

These are all covered, in the following pages.

If people are making a nuisance of themselves

If you or your organisation becomes a 'story' you may have people camped on your doorstep for 24 hours, or making it impossible for your advice centre to function by pestering your clients.

The best way to send them away may be to give them the information they are interested in, but in the form, and to the extent, that *you* want. Issue a news release, or hold a news conference (see Chapter 17–18). If the topic goes on being of interest to the media, do so again – every day, if necessary. Otherwise, the only other statement you need to make is, 'We have given you information. We have no other comment.'

Make a note of the behaviour you find offensive, or that is disrupting your work or your private life, and let the journalists know that you are doing it. Contact their editors, or their senior managers, as explained above. Ask them to prevent the journalists acting in this way. If this fails, go to one of the bodies listed above.

Alternatively, ask the police or a solicitor to intervene, under the law.

Using the law

There is no law of privacy in this country, but there are other parts of the law that *may* help.

Trespass
People are not allowed onto your private property without your permission. You can eject them, using only what force is necessary. Be careful if doing this, as the other person might sue for assault. You can also threaten them with an injunction, and if necessary take one out. If there is any damage to your property, you can threaten to sue for damages. (In Scotland there is no law of trespass, but you can still sue if your property is damaged.)

Obstruction
This is a matter for the police, not the individual. They can order someone to stop blocking the road or the footpath, and arrest them if they do not. How sympathetic the police are will depend on what the issue is, what they feel about your group, and how worried they are about getting bad publicity themselves. Call the police as soon as people start making a nuisance of themselves. Even if they claim they can't do anything, you will not have lost anything.

Neither of these laws can stop *publication* of the information that they collect by this means. But you might be able to use the law of confidence, the Theft Act, or an injunction, in the ways that were explained in Chapter 10. Think about the consequences in terms of publicity for your organisation, and the effect on your supporters, before doing so.

Going to outside bodies

There are several organisations to whom you can complain about what has been said or written about you. None is very effective, but because the law of libel (explained on page 106) is so difficult to deal with, you will normally be better to start the process by going to one of them. If you think it is likely that you will end up in court, take legal advice from the beginning. Ask a solicitor to draft the letter for you. You should be able to get this advice free or cheaply, under the Green Form scheme.

The NUJ code
Probably the least useful to you is the code of guidance of the National Union of Journalists (NUJ). A number of newspaper and magazine publishers have refused recognition to the NUJ, or withdrawn it, so the offending journalist may not be a member. Even where there is an agreement, the workplace group (called a Chapel) may not be very strong, or the individual concerned may choose to take no notice. So

Figure 21.1

THE NUJ CODE

1. A journalist has a duty to maintain the highest professional and ethical standards.

2. A journalist shall at all times defend the principle of the freedom of the press and other media in relation to the collection of information and the expression of comment and criticism. He/she shall strive to eliminate distortion, news suppression and censorship.

3. A journalist shall strive to ensure that the information he/she disseminates is fair and accurate, avoid the expression of comment and conjecture as established fact and falsification by distortion, selection or misrepresentation.

4. A journalist shall rectify promptly any harmful inaccuracies, ensure that correction and apologies receive due prominence, and afford the right of reply to persons criticised when the issue is of sufficient importance.

5. A journalist shall obtain information, photographs and illustrations only by straightforward means. The use of other means can be justified only by overriding considerations of the public interest. The journalist is entitled to exercise a personal conscientious objection to the use of such means.

6. Subject to the justification by overriding considerations of the public interest, a journalist shall do nothing which entails intrusion into private grief and distress.

7. A journalist shall protect confidential sources of information.

8. A journalist shall not accept bribes nor shall he/she allow other inducements to influence the performance of his/her professional duties.

9. A journalist shall not lend him/herself to the distortion or suppression of the truth because of advertising or other considerations.

10. A journalist shall only mention a person's race, colour, creed, illegitimacy, disability, marital status (or lack of it), gender or sexual orientation if this information is strictly relevant. A journalist shall neither originate nor process material which encourages discrimination on any of the above-mentioned grounds.

11. A journalist shall not take private advantage of information gained in the course of his/her duties, before the information is public knowledge.

12. A journalist shall not by way of statement, voice or appearance endorse by advertisement any commercial product or service save for the promotion of his/her own work, or of the medium by which he/she is employed.

although the Code of Conduct looks good on paper, it only has moral force, and there is little power behind it.

You can obtain a copy of the Code from the NUJ (see Appendix 2: Addresses). Its twelve points are listed in Figure 21.1.

The Editors' Code of Practice

Figure 21.2

THE EDITORS' CODE OF PRACTICE*

We, the editors of all Britain's national newspapers, declare our determination to defend the democratic right of the people to a Press free from government interference.

[...]

Editors have agreed on a common code of practice and the establishment of systems of ombudsmen to take up complaints and breaches of the code. The ombudsmen's authority will be set out in formal terms of reference.

They will safeguard standards of accuracy, fairness and the conduct of journalists.

They will have the power to question journalists and editorial executives. They will have the right to require prompt publication of statements of correction and to have their findings published.

If a dispute cannot be settled in this way, the right to appeal to the Press Complaints Commission, of course, remains.

The Code
RESPECT FOR PRIVACY: Intrusion into private lives should always have a public interest justification;
OPPORTUNITY FOR REPLY: A fair opportunity for reply will be given when reasonably called for;
PROMPT CORRECTIONS: Mistakes will be corrected promptly and with appropriate prominence;
CONDUCT OF JOURNALISTS: Subject only to the existence of an overriding public interest, information for publication will be obtained by straightforward means. Similarly, newspapers will not authorise payment to criminals or their families and associates to enable them to profit from crime.
RACE, COLOUR: Irrelevant references to race, colour and religion will be avoided.

---

* This is a shortened version; the paragraphs that are not relevant here have been left out. The newspapers have adopted slightly different versions of the code itself. Source: *British Journalism Review*, Winter 1990.

This was agreed in 1989 by all the editors of the national newspapers (except *Sunday Sport*), mainly because they were being threatened with legislation on the subject. They have each appointed 'readers' representatives' or 'ombudsmen' who are supposed to be independent people who can take up readers' complaints. The names of the papers' ombudsmen should be printed in the paper each day, with a note of how to contact him or her.

The Press Complaints Commission

This replaced the old Press Council at the beginning of 1991. It was set up voluntarily by the newspaper editors, to prove that they did not need government legislation to control them. It is heavily dominated by the editors. It has a code of practice, reproduced in Figure 21.3.

You complain by writing to the Commission at 1 Salisbury Square, London EC4Y 8AE.

It will deal with complaints entirely in writing, and so things could be quite long winded. (The old Press Council could take months or years.) However, since the editors themselves have set it up, one hopes that they will take it seriously. However, the time and trouble involved, and the unlikelihood of winning, all make it pretty unattractive to a small campaigning group.

The Broadcasting Complaints Commission

This is roughly the equivalent body for TV and radio. It started in 1981, and has made very little impact on the public so far. It can only consider complaints about:

- Unfair or unjust treatment in radio or TV programmes actually broadcast by a body, or included in a licensed cable programme service (not satellite TV).
- Unwarranted infringement of privacy in, or in connection with, obtaining material included in such programmes.

Individuals and organisations can both complain, but they must have a personal involvement. That is, they must feel they themselves to have been treated unfairly or their privacy to have been infringed. You have to complain in writing, and can do so either directly or after going to the broadcasting body and not getting satisfaction. But if there are legal proceedings (like a libel action) going on, the Commission can't hear your complaint. They can also say that you have delayed too long, or that your complaint is frivolous.

If they decide to look at a complaint, they ask the relevant broadcasting authority to send them a transcript of the programme concerned, and a written answer to the complaint. Then they ask the person who has complained for another written response, and ask the broadcasters

Figure 21.3
THE PRESS COMPLAINTS COMMISSION CODE OF PRACTICE

The Press Complaints Commission are charged with enforcing the following Code of Practice which was framed by the newspaper and periodical industry.

All members of the Press have a duty to maintain the highest professional and ethical standards. In doing so, they should have regard to the provisions of this code of practice and to safeguarding the people's right to know.

Editors are responsible for the actions of journalists employed by their publications. They should also satisfy themselves as far as possible that material accepted from non-staff members was obtained in accordance with this code.

While recognising that this involves a substantial element of self-restraint by editors and journalists, it is designed to be acceptable in the context of a system of self-regulation. The code applies in the spirit as well as in the letter.

1. **Accuracy**
   (i) Newspapers and periodicals should take care not to publish inaccurate, misleading or distorted material.
   (ii) Whenever it is recognised that a significant inaccuracy, misleading statement or distorted report has been published it should be corrected promptly and with due prominence.
   (iii) An apology should be published whenever appropriate.
   (iv) A newspaper or periodical should always report fairly and accurately the outcome of an action for defamation to which it has been a party.

2. **Opportunity to reply**
   A fair opportunity for reply to inaccuracies should be given to individuals or organisations when reasonably called for.

3. **Comment, conjecture and fact**
   Newspapers, while free to be partisan, should distinguish clearly between comment, conjecture and fact.

4. **Privacy**
   Intrusions and enquiries into an individual's private life without his or her consent are not generally acceptable and publication can only be justified when in the public interest. This would include:
   (i) Detecting or exposing crime or serious misdemeanour.
   (ii) Detecting or exposing seriously anti-social conduct.
   (iii) Protecting public health and safety.
   (iv) Preventing the public from being misled by some statement or action of that individual.

5. **Hospitals**
   (i) Journalists or photographers making enquiries at hospitals or similar institutions should identify themselves to a responsible official and obtain

permission before entering non-public areas.

(ii) The restrictions on intruding into privacy are particularly relevant to enquiries about individuals in hospital or similar institutions.

6. Misrepresentation

(i) Journalists should not generally obtain or seek to obtain information or pictures through misrepresentation or subterfuge.

(ii) Unless in the public interest, documents or photographs should be removed only with the express consent of the owner.

(iii) Subterfuge can be justified only in the public interest and only when material cannot be obtained by any other means. In all these clauses the public interest includes:

(a) Detecting or exposing crime or serious misdemeanour.

(b) Detecting or exposing anti-social conduct.

(c) Protecting public health and safety.

(d) Preventing the public from being misled by some statement or action of that individual or organisation.

7. Harassment

(i) Journalists should neither obtain information nor pictures through intimidation or harassment.

(ii) Unless their enquiries are in the public interest, journalists should not photograph individuals on private property without their consent; should not persist in telephoning or questioning individuals after having been asked to desist; should not remain on their property after having been asked to leave and should not follow them.

The public interest will include:

(a) Detecting or exposing crime or serious misdemeanour.

(b) Detecting or exposing anti-social conduct.

(c) Protecting public health and safety.

(d) Preventing the public from being misled by some statement or action of that individual or organisation.

8. Payment for articles

(i) Payments or offers of payment for stories, pictures or information should not be made to witnesses or potential witnesses in current criminal proceedings or to people engaged in crime or to their associates except where the material concerned ought to be published in the public interest and the payment is necessary for this to be done.

The public interest will include:

(a) Detecting or exposing crime or serious misdemeanour.

(b) Detecting or exposing anti-social conduct.

(c) Protecting public health and safety.

(d) Preventing the public from being misled by some

statement or action of that individual or organisation.

(ii) "Associates" include family, friends, neighbours and colleagues.

(iii) Payments should not be made either directly or indirectly through agents.

9. Intrusion into grief or shock

In cases involving personal grief or shock, enquiries should be carried out and approaches made with sympathy and discretion.

10. Innocent relatives and friends

The Press should generally avoid identifying relatives or friends of persons convicted or accused of crime unless the reference to them is necessary for the full, fair and accurate reporting of the crime or legal proceedings.

11. Interviewing or photographing children

(i) Journalists should not normally interview or photograph children under the age of 16 on subjects involving the personal welfare of the child, in the absence of or without the consent of a parent or other adult who is responsible for the children.

(ii) Children should not be approached or photographed while at school without the permission of the school authorities.

12. Children in sex cases

The Press should not, even where the law does not prohibit it, identify children under the age of 16 who are involved in cases concerning sexual offences, whether as victims, or as witnesses or defendants.

13. Victims of crime

The Press should not identify victims of sexual assault or publish material likely to contribute to such identification unless, by law, they are free to do so.

14. Discrimination

(i) The Press should avoid prejudicial or pejorative reference to a person's race, colour, religion, sex or sexual orientation or to any physical or mental illness or handicap.

(ii) It should avoid publishing details of a person's race, colour, religion, sex or sexual orientation, unless these are directly relevant to the story.

15. Financial journalism

(i) Even where the law does not prohibit it, journalists should not use for their own profit financial information they receive in advance of its general publication nor should they pass such information to others.

(ii) They should not write about shares or securities in whose performance they know that they or their close families have a significant financial interest, without disclosing the interest to the editor or financial editor.

(iii) They should not buy or sell, either directly or through nominees or agents, shares or securities about which they have written recently or about which they intend to write in the near future.

16. Confidential sources

Journalists have a moral obligation to protect confidential sources of information.

---

to respond to that. Sometimes they arrange a private hearing and invite both sides, or they can ask each side to appear before them separately.

When they have decided on their views, they make an adjudication in writing, and send it to the broadcasting body and the person complaining. A summary of it is then broadcast, and published in the *Radio Times* or *TV Times*. But the Commission can't make the broadcasters publish a correction or an apology, or provide compensation.

Their address is in Appendix 2: Addresses.

Taking a libel action

The law on libel was explained on page 106. If you decide you have no alternative but to take action, go first to a solicitor and ask whether you have been libelled under the law, and what your chances are of winning a case. You cannot get legal aid for this.

The next stage is to send a letter threatening a libel action. This may be enough to force a retraction and apology. If not, you may need to issue a writ. All these stages could take two or three years, but if you carry on pursuing the case, it will eventually come to court. There will be an effort by the other side to persuade you to drop the matter, or to reach an out of court settlement. If the others know that they were in the wrong, and that it will hurt their reputation if the case comes to court, they may be willing to offer quite a large sum of money, and to pay your legal costs. But you are involved in a gamble here: on the one hand, you may feel that your case is so good that a settlement should be a great deal higher than is offered; on the other, you could lose, or be offered only nominal damages (explained on page 108) and end up paying heavy legal costs, both for yourself and for the other side.

If there is no settlement, then at some point you will have to decide whether to go ahead with a court hearing or not. Withdrawing will mean that you have to pay your own legal costs so far, and possibly the other side's also – though this may be negotiable.

If in the end you decide you cannot pursue the matter, issue a dignified statement saying that you have withdrawn, but that you still consider the original statement was untrue and unfair.

Appendix 1: Booklist

Writers' and Artists' Yearbook, A & C Black, 1992

Advertising by Charities, Ken Burnett (ed), Directory of Social Change, 1986

Data Protection Guidance for Advertising and Marketing, Data Protection Registrar, June 1991

Get It On, Jane Drinkwater, Pluto Press, 1984

Marketing Handbook: a Guide for Voluntary and Non-Profit Making Organisations, Rosalind Druce and Stephen Carter, National Extension College, 1989

Lobbying, Alf Dubs, Pluto Press, 1988

Editing, Design and Book Production, Charles Foster, Journeyman Press, 1992

What News? The Market, Politics and the Local Press, Bob Franklin and David Murphy, Routledge, 1991

McNae's Essential Law for Journalists (11th edition), W Greenwood and T Welsh, Butterworths, London, 1990

News in the Regions: Plymouth Sound to Moray Firth, Alastair Hetherington, Macmillan, 1989

Illustrated Guide to Employee Reports, Industrial Society, 1984

Getting Your Message Across, Barbara Lowndes, National Federation of Community Organisations, 1989

Preaching to the Converted?: Trade Unions and Video, ACCT/North East Media Development Council, 1988 (now available from BECTU)

NUJ Members' Handbook, National Union of Journalists, 1989

Charities & Broadcasting, N Parker (ed), Directory of Social Change, 1988

'The Nestlé Boycott', *Public Relations*, Winter 1985

Public Relations in Practice, Public Relations Consultants Association, 1991

Freelances and Computers: A General Guide on the Potential Health Hazards of Using Computer Terminals, A Rowe, National Union of Journalists, 1989

They Aren't in the Brief: Advertising People with Disabilities, Susan Scott Parker, King's Fund, December 1989

Marketing for Small Publishers, Bill Godber, Keith Smith and Robert Webb, Journeyman Press, 1992

Lessons of the Sogat Ballot, SOGAT, May 1989 (now available from BECTU)

Meeting the Corporate Challenge, Transnationals Information Exchange, February 1985

A–Z of Meetings, Sue Ward, Pluto Press, 1983

Organising Things: A Guide to Successful Political Action, Sue Ward, Pluto Press, 1984

Pressure: The A-Z of Campaigning in Britain, Des Wilson, Heinemann, 1984

Print: How You Can Do It Yourself, Jonathan Zeitlyn, Journeyman Press, 1992

Effective Publicity and Design, Jonathan Zeitlyn, InterChange Books, 1989

Children in the Picture, Stephanie Tebbutt (ed), Journeyman Press, 1992

Appendix 2: Addresses

ActionMatch, c/o Community Links, Canning Town Public Hall, 105 Barking Road, London E16 4HQ

BECTU, 111 Wardour Street, London W1V 4AY

Broadcasting Complaints Commission, Grosvenor Gardens House, 35 & 37 Grosvenor Gardens, London SW1W 0BS (Tel; 071 630 1966)

Child Poverty Action Group (CPAG), 1–5 Bath Street, London EC1V 9PY

Community Computing Network, 5 Riverains, 71 Vicarage Crescent, London SW11 3UN

Data Protection Registrar, Springfield House, Water Lane, Wilmslow, Cheshire SK9 5AX

Graphical Media and Paper Union (GMPU), Keys House, 63–67 Bromham Road, Bedford MK40 2AG (formerly SOGAT and NGA)

Liberty, 21 Tabard Street, London SE1 4LA (formerly National Council for Civil Liberties)

National Union of Journalists, Acorn House, 314–320 Grays Inn Road, London WC1X 8DP

North East Media Development Council, Norden House, 41 Stowell Street, Newcastle upon Tyne NE1 1YB

Poster Marketing, Centric House, 230 Strand, London WC2

Press Association, 85 Fleet Street, London EC4

Press Complaints Commission, 1 Salisbury Square, London EC4Y 8AE

Shelter, 88 Old Street, London EC1V 9HU

Standard Book Numbering Agency, 12 Dyott Street, London WC1A 1DF

TUC, Congress House, Great Russell Street, London WC1B 3LS

The Volunteer Centre, 29 lower Kings Road, Berkhamsted, Herts HP4 2AB

A few sources of media training (this is not an exhaustive list) are:

Veronica Creighton, 30 Cookham Road, London SW6 4EQ

Industrial Society, Robert Hyde House, 48 Bryanston Square, London SW1H 7LN

Interchange Trust, Dalby Street, Kentish Town, London NW3 3NQ

Research Training Initiatives, 18–20 Dean Street, Newcastle upon Tyne NE1 1PG

Index

labels, 144, 150
lapel stickers, 40
laser printer, 83, 94, 95, 97; *see also* printers
launch event, 37
Law, 104, 111, 121, 220; of Confidence, 111–12, 221; of Privacy, 220, 222–3; legal action, 213; legal advice, 106, 109–10, 220, 227; *see also* defamation, libel,
layout, 82–4, 90, 92–3, 137–8, 182, 206
leaflets, 3–4, 8, 13, 17–18, 20, 22, 27–8, 30, 32, 40–41, 42, 44, 49, 64, 71, 73, 75, 82–4, 117, 119, 131–2, 135, 143, 151, 153–4, 157, 159, 169, 200, 214
leak of information, 110, 113
letters, 13, 24, 27, 29, 34, 38, 40, 41, 43, 45–7, 79, 106, 146, 150, 218, *see also* direct mail; page, 34, 165, 201–2 *see also* newspapers
libel, 106–10, 113, 218–19, 220, 223–7
Liberty, 110, 112–13
library, 123, 135, 145, 156, 158, 166, 168, 170, 176, 198
linespacing, 90
lobbying, 62, 70, 127, 146
local newspapers, *see* newspapers; radio
location work, 157 *see* videos
logo, 125–6, 141, 190, 196, 206, 210

magazines, 32, 33, 34, 44, 76, 105, 124, 127, 132, 135–42, 145, 163, 165, 167, 169; controlled circulation, 165; specialist magazines, 165, 166, 204, 214; women's, 168, 175
mail order, 126, 132, 159 *see also* direct mail
mailing house *see* direct mail; list, 27, 29, 32, 47, 132, 144, 147–8
mailings, 39, 147, 159
major story, 170, 181
margins, 87, 90, 96
mark up, 94, 131, 133 *see also* copy
market research, 149, 172

marketing, 131
masthead, 140
media, 132, 135, 147, 163, 166, 172–3, 176, 189, 191, 198, 217; buying agency, 125; directories, 125; officer, 176–7, 181, 194, 197, 200, 213; pack, 191, 196–7
meetings, 24, 69, 70–1, 73, 142, 158, branch, 35; chairing, 73
membership, 39, 43, 63, 119, 151, 153, 157; card, 82; charge, 44; form, 39; leaflets, 71
message, 12, 17, 22, 27–9, 32, 35–7, 39, 68–9, 81, 117, 120–1, 140, 153, 156, 166, 199, 210; negative, 20; positive, 20, 23
misrepresentation, 194, 217–18, 221, *see also* complaints
mission statement, 7
mistakes, 217–19 *see also* complaints
monitoring, 171, 176, 193
morale, 32
mouse, 97, *see also* computer
MPs, 12, 28, 44, 48, 69, 107, 174 *see* politicians

national newspapers, *see* newspapers
National Union of Journalists (NUJ), 78, 220
new projects, 37; supporters, 24
news conference, 188, 194–5, 219; programmes *see* radio and TV programmes; release, 17, 35, 38–9, 43, 47–8, 70–71, 128, 131, 134, 159, 168–70, 173–6, 178–84, 187–9, 193–4, 196–200, 207, 214, 219; stories, 28, 33, 35, 143
newsagents, 145, 165, 167
newsletter, 4, 13, 17, 22, 24–5, 28, 32, 75–7 1 93, 117, 135–6, 214
newspapers, 21–2, 32, 33, 34, 39, 44, 47, 83 , 93, 105, 127, 138 163–6, 172, 178–9, 184, 189, 190, 195, 200; local 33, 48; qualities, 138, 163, 166, 201, 219; regional, 164, 167; tabloid, 83, 164, 166, 175; weekly, 223
newspoints, 138